Áine Flanagan Productions and Seiriol Davies present

HOW TO WIN AGAINST HISTORY

Book, Music and Lyrics by Seiriol Davies
Directed by Alex Swift
Devised by The Company

Seiriol Davies

Seiriol Davies is a composer, writer and performer from Anglesey. He trained with Thomas Prattki at LISPA, and has made work with companies like Punchdrunk, You Need Me, One Tenth Human, Giant Bird, Kristin Fredricksson & Beady Eye, Rififi and Boileroom, with whom he won the Oxford Samuel Beckett Theatre Trust Award. *Mess*, which he created with Caroline Horton & Co, premiered at the Traverse, Edinburgh in 2012, winning awards including The Stage Award for Acting Excellence and an Argus Angel. He was Cyril Millions in the cult retro-punk time-travelling music hall act Underbling & Vow, wrote and performed with Weimar-glam art band Temper Temper and was a founder member of the Brighton-based performance collective Beatabet.

Alex Swift – Director

Alex Swift is a performer, director and theatre-maker. He trained at École Philippe Gaulier in Paris and his work has won Best Ensemble in the Stage Awards for Acting Excellence, The Bush Theatre Directing Award, The Vault Pick of the Festival Award and an Argus Angel. He is also Artistic Director of Permanent Red Theatre Company and an Associate Artist with Daedalus Theatre Company. Recent work as director includes *An Injury* by Kieran Hurley, *Instructions for Border Crossing* by Daniel Bye, *Heads Up* by Kieran Hurley, *Me and Mr C* by Gary Kitching, *Error 404* by Daniel Bye, *Fat Man* by Martin Bonger, *Mess* by Caroline Horton, *Puffball* by Caroline Williams, and *I Told You This Would Happen* by Kathryn Beaumont. He developed his solo show, *Travesty*, at Theatre in The Mill, Bradford.

Matthew Blake – Performer / Co-Deviser

Matthew trained as a theatre maker and actor at East 15 under Brian Astbury. He regularly writes and directs for Punchdrunk and has created shows with Hijinx, Gideon Reeling and Battersea Arts Centre, and has been nominated for Welsh National Award for Best Director and Best English Language Production. Acting theatre credits include; Larry Fortune/Mr Tuttle in *The Drowned Man: A Hollywood Fable* directed by Felix Barrett and Maxine Doyle (Punchdrunk/National Theatre), Matt in *Bank On It* directed by Sue Buckmaster (Theatre Rites/Barbican), Mr Winter in *The House Where Winter Lives* directed by Peter Higgin (Punchdrunk), Momentologist in *The Good Neighbour* directed by Sarah Golding (Battersea Arts Centre), M Gould in *Starty* (Soho Theatre and Shoreditch Town Hall). Matthew performed in and co-devised the 2016 Edinburgh Fringe sell-out *How to Win Against History*, which won The Stage Edinburgh Award and a Broadway Baby Bobby.

Dylan Townley – Performer / Musical Director

Dylan trained as an actor-musician and improviser while at Oxford University. Credits include sell-out tours of Australia and Europe as MD of long-form improvisation troupe Racing Minds; co-creator and multi-instrumentalist of acclaimed duo Peablossom Cabaret; MD and cast member of *Thumbelina* UK tour and Orpheus in *Jason and the Argonauts* with Dancing Brick; composer and MD of *Jack Drum's Entertainment* and National Theatre Connections play *The Monstrum* with the Young Actors Company, Cambridge; pianist in the 'Whose Line Is It Anyway?' and hypnosis mash-up *Hyprov*; co-creator of *Adventures of the Improvised Sherlock Holmes*; writer for the hit online channel *History Bombs*; and MD and performer with 2016 Edinburgh Fringe sell-out *How to Win Against History*, which won The Stage Edinburgh Award and a Broadway Baby Bobby. He arranged the score of the show, which is published by Oberon Books.

Verity Quinn – Designer

Verity is an award-nominated theatre designer who trained at Nottingham Trent. Recent design credits include: *How to Win Against History* Tour 2017 (Seiriol Davies & Áine Flanagan Productions); *The Borrowers* (Polka Theatre); *Vinegar Tom* (RADA); *Getting Dressed* (Second Hand Dance); *Laika, Baby Show, Septimus Bean and His Amazing Machine, Once Upon A Christmas; The Fourth Wise Man, Seesaw, When I Think About the Universe I Laugh For No Reason* and *Dora* (Unicorn Theatre); *Dame Nature* (Tim Bell & Havoc Theatre); *How To Win Against History* (Áine Flanagan Productions); *Under the Rainbow* (Polka Theatre); *Holy Mackerel* (Eastern Angles); *Beasty Baby* (Theatre-Rites & Polka Theatre); *Alpha Beta* (Finborough Theatre); *Free* (Half Moon Theatre); *Blue Boy* (New Writing North & Northern Stage); *Apples* (Company of Angels & Northern Stage); *The Girls from Poppyfield Close* (Live Theatre); *Heartbreak Soup* (The Empty Space & Laura Lindow)

Dan Saggars – Lighting Designer

Dan studied at Middlesex University in Lighting Design and Technical Theatre. He designs many types of performance including theatre, opera and dance. Design credits include: *How To Win Against History Tour 2017* (Seiriol Davies and Áine Flanagan Productions), *Punts* at Theatre503, *The Borrowers* at Polka Theatre, *Orfeo et Euridice, Alcina* and *Xerxes* at Longborough Festival Opera, *Carry On Jaywick* at Vaults Festival and touring, Laura Lindow's *Then Leap!* at The Lowry, Manchester and rural touring, *Echo_Narcissus* at The Yard Theatre, *The Lamellar Project* at South Hill Park Studio and UK Touring for Alex Marshall Design, *Vanity Fair* at Middle Temple Hall, *Only Forever* at The Hope Theatre, *The Three Musketeers* at Kenton Theatre and *Bernarda Alba* at The Cockpit Theatre.

Eve Leigh – Dramaturg

Eve is a playwright and theatremaker. Her play *Spooky Action at a Distance* was the 2017 Royal Court/RWCMD commission, performed at the Burton Theatre, Cardiff, and the Gate Theatre, London. She has had two full-length plays on at the Finborough Theatre: *Silent Planet* and *Stone Face*. *Stone Face* was shortlisted for three Offies, including Best New Play. Other plays include *The Curtain* (Young Vic Taking Part), *Plunder* (Young Vic Taking Part), *Red Sky at Night* (Bush Theatre), *Rapture* (Soho Theatre), *The Trick* (Teatr Polski Bydgoszcz).

Interactive installations include *The Voice of the House* (Duppini Art Group/ Studio Я Maxim Gorki Theater), *Your Future* (Camden People's Theatre, Hebbel Am Ufer, Ballhaus Ost, and Sophiensaele), *A Short and Boring Story* (Camden People's Theatre). Upcoming work includes commissions from the Royal Shakespeare Company and a residency at the Experimental Stage of the National Theatre of Greece.

Bert Roman – Movement Director

Bert finished his Bachelor's Degree in contemporary dance at the conservatoire in Antwerp, Belgium, and was awarded a scholarship for Danceweb as part of Impulstanz 2009 in Vienna. The companies he has danced for include; United-c, De Maan, Andwhatbeside(s)death, Cacao blue and Joji Inc. His movement director experience includes projects for: La Monnaie/De Munt National Opera Brussels, Temple Theatre, Theatre Temoin, Single Shoe Productions, Mountview Academy of Theatre Arts, London Fashion Week and pop band Friss.be. He also coaches individual performers in the development of their own work and teaches movement based workshops.

Bert is a founding member of international theatre ensemble Babakas. He was also part of the team that founded and developed Birmingham's international theatre festival, BE FESTIVAL. As an experienced project manager and events producer, Bert is now artistic director, choreographer and founder of MoveMe Dance, a London based company producing MoveMe, a participatory dance event. Unusual fact: Before studying dance Bert completed his degree as a Nurse.

Áine Flanagan Productions

Current productions include: *How to Win Against History*, by Seiriol Davies, *Margaret Thatcher Queen of Soho* and *Margaret Thatcher Queen of Game Shows* by Jon Brittain and Matthew Tedford. She is also currently developing Rebecca Humphries' new musical *Prom Kween*, Seiriol Davies' new show *Milky Peaks* and *Hear Me Raw* by Daniella Isaacs, all of which will be launched in 2018.

Áine is proudly supported by the Stage One Bursary Scheme for new Producers.
www.aineflanagan.com

Special Thanks

Tom Penn, our first Band, for being a huge part of creating the music and joy.

Thank you to

Dickie Andrews,
Marie Arnold,
Rebecca Atkinson-Lord,
Emily Austen,
Sandy B,
Tom Ball,
Rachel Briscoe,
Daniel Bye,
Owen Calvert-Lyons,
Vera Chok,
Ed Collier,
Maria O'Connor,
Amy Cooke-Hodgson,
Eleri Cwyfan,
Mair Glynne Davies,
Clare Dunn,
Lily Einhorn,
Sylvie Einhorn,
Jude Einhorn,
Lucy Ellinson,
Gareth Llŷr Evans,
Ciara Flanagan,
Eamon Flanagan,
Viv Gardner,
Gareth Glyn,
Christopher Green,
Christopher Haydon,

Amy Hewett,
Petra Hjortsberg,
Dafydd Cwyfan Hughes,
Luke Kilgarriff,
Bryony Kimmings,
Lisa Lee,
Cassandra Mathers,
Roisin and Eoghan O'Connor Flanagan,
everyone at Ovalhouse,
Charlie Penn,
Matthew Poxon,
Rachel May Snider,
Rob Stothard,
Lily Sykes,
Christopher Sykes,
Rich Thomas,
Simon Townley,
Sue Vermes,
Julia Voce,
Peredur Glyn Webb-Davies,
Kelly Webb-Davies,
Brython Webb-Davies,
Paul Warwick,
Deborah Williams,
John Williams,
Lily Williams

And Henry Cyril Paget. Massively. Obvs.

The 2016 production of *How to Win Against History* was supported by Cyngor Celfeddydau Cymru, Arts Council England, Theatr Pontio, Bangor, and Ovalhouse, London. It toured in 2017 as a co-production with the Young Vic.

Henry's birthday do, 1902. Henry's in the middle in the dress (naturally), and behind him is Mr Keith. This photo reproduced by the grace of Prof. Viv Gardner.

by Seiriol Davies

Annotated script edition

OBERON BOOKS
LONDON

WWW.OBERONBOOKS.COM

First published in 2017 by Oberon Books Ltd
521 Caledonian Road, London N7 9RH
Tel: +44 (0) 20 7607 3637 / Fax: +44 (0) 20 7607 3629
e-mail: info@oberonbooks.com
www.oberonbooks.com

A catalogue record for this book is available from the British Library.

PB ISBN: 9781786822406
E ISBN: 9781786822413

Cover photo by Damien Frost
Designed by Konstantinos Vasdekis

Printed and bound by 4edge Limited, Essex, UK.
eBook conversion by CPI Group (UK) Ltd, Croydon, CR0 4YY.

Visit www.oberonbooks.com to read more about all our books and to
buy them. You will also find features, author interviews and news of
any author events, and you can sign up for e-newsletters so that you're
always first to hear about our new releases.

Regrettably: A Foreword

I grew up on Ynys Mon, a.k.a. Anglesey, a.k.a. The Druidic Haven of the Celts, a.k.a. The Flat Bit Before You Get To The Irish Ferry. It's a barreny, lovely, salty sort of place. Henry Cyril Paget also lived there, which is handy.

While we've been making *HTWAH*, I've said this particular story so many times that I've a bit lost track of exactly how true it is (oh my god look: thematic relevance), but my recollection is I used to make my parents take me to *Plas Newydd*, which is the Paget family's estate on Anglesey, over and over again as a boy. Of course, it may have been like twice and I just sucked it all in through my hungry, mad child-eyes in such detail that it felt like loads. And I should say it's a National Trust place, we didn't just turn up at somebody's house with me in the back seat, goggle-eyed and absorbing key memories for later musical theatre projects.

In fact, my mum has in her retirement expressed an interest in working at Plas Newydd and becoming one of those powerful-looking National Trust ladies who dwell by the fireplaces in an angora cardie waiting to tell you what that weird Game of Thronesy thing is (it's probably a long-range bedpan) or to point vehemently at the 'stop prodding that' sign, or to pose for the odd awkward group selfie with a family in velourette anoraks from Wisconsin. And I for one think this would be very exciting.

But anyway, there were two key reasons why I wanted to go there so much:

(i) The mural by painter Rex Whistler (the non-*Whistler's Mother* one) which is all Italianate froufferies and phantastickal towers and harbour-folk, and is well worth the twenty minute tour guide talk-through, as it does things with foreshortening that beggar belief. Like, if you as a viewer do a nifty crab-walk along the floor in front of it, it can make a sailboat seem to sail out of the harbour before your very eyes while not moving at all in real life because it is a painting and this is not Harry Potter. Or at least, that is what the tour guide claimed, and my response was to just glare at it until I could sufficiently motivate myself to believe I could see what she was talking about.

But in any case, it's a bit *Where's Wally* and a bit *Magic Eye* and I was so preoccupied with it that we've now got a framed copy of it up by the sink in the kitchen in my flat. And I'm fairly sure that, if it wasn't positioned where the glassware cupboard door slammed into it with alarming enthusiasm every time I open it, I would have by now found the peace to enter its zone and divine its secrets while washing the wine glasses of a Tuesday morning. But, as it is, I just get mesmerised and accidentally smack it again with the cupboard door.

(b) The small collection of laminated, photocopied snaps of Henry Cyril which were grudgingly stuck on the wall next to the toilet by the back porch. Now, as context, the pictures of the other, preceding Marquises (NB Other people seem to say 'Marquess', but I tend to prefer 'Marquis'. I'm not sure why; I think maybe cos Henry seemed to favour it that way, and I'm just some ratbag socialisty commoner with Radio 4 affectations, so I've allowed myself to pick which spelling I fancied. Do get in touch, *DeBrett's*) are not exhibited in the same laminatey toilet zone; their pictures are painted in oil, hanging in big gold frames in rooms you actually hang out in, or they are immortalised as busts, or full-body statues on top of huge columns erected looming over Llanfairpwllgwyngyllgogerychwyrndrobwllllantysiliogogogoch (a nearby village) as a deliberate copying of Nelson's Column in London.

Well, one of them has that. The first Marquis was a hero at the battle of Waterloo (by which we presumably mean he stood in a big hat at the back telling some poor people to run that way) and was *so* British that, when his leg got blown off by a cannon shell, The Duke of Wellington, who was next to him, looked down and said "By Jove, sir, I think your leg's been blown off" and Paget looked down and said "By Jove, sir, I think you're right". For these services to hats, shouting and limb-removal-not-noticing, he got himself a Column, which is probably one of NW Wales's top Columns, and I really mean that.

The fact that it was this sort of lineage Henry Cyril was coming from makes it no real surprise that he got relegated to the Gallery De Toilette, because... I mean look at him. Google Image Search 'Henry Cyril Paget' and look at them outfits.

Aren't they stu-*hunn*-ing? Doesn't he look like Freddie Mercury drove through Elizabeth Duke's wearing a sellotape suit?

I drank them in, those pictures, though not really identifying very much with the whole fabulousness thing. I've never been an extravagant dresser per se, apart from a brief phase when I took to tying bright scarves to the belt loops of my skater jeans in an attempt to look like a sort of sexy satyr, but ended up looking (as a friend helpfully pointed out) "as though my butt was wearing a cape". And, at the time of seeing the images, I was probably wearing a Homer Simpson T-shirt, urban camo trousers and Hi-Tecs.

But there's just something about him in those pictures. Okay, sure, there's the millions of poundsworth of costume budget; but there's also the sort of *'don't give a fig'* attitude he has which I loved: that he's gazing out, dressed for some reason as a prog rock chandelier, telling the world to fig off, the bunch of motherfiggers.

And reading the little inscription underneath, which said (spoiler alert) that he'd ruined himself, died young and been expunged from the family history as comprehensively as possible – with all the letters, photos and diaries his family could find, burnt – set off my little internal bell of moral outrage. And so, because I believe in swift, decisive action, I decided to make a play about it twenty years later.

But over all that time, the simplicity of that feeling hasn't really changed, despite growing-upness making it clear the whole thing's more complicated, what with issues of privilege and stuff like that.

Because that's Henry. Even though on paper he's not the most obviously sympathetic character ("Hey come see my show about this dead white millionaire and how hard his life was. Come back please!") people have just seemed to warm to him. Due to some combination of his defiance, his outsideryness writ on such a massive, Imperial scale and the fact that we know hardly anything about his internal life (due to the aforementioned bonfire), people seem to be able to pour themselves into him. Because I reckon most of us, at least some of the time, think we're an outsider in a world that everyone else gets. And whatever our actual ambitions, very few of us are quite so extravagantly emo as to want no trace of us to exist after death.

Also yes, his outfits are life-giving.

I wanted to make something that redressed the balance a tiny bit; that told at least a version of his story as pieced together from a lot of extraordinary events with no internal monologue. With songs and me in a dress and a gag about Keira Knightley.

However, the truth is: there is a bit more stuff that survived the fire. I was lucky enough to have the help of Lily and Christopher Sykes, who are descendants of the actual real life Lilian from her second marriage, as well as Prof Viv Gardner, fabulous performance historian at the University of Manchester. With their help – as well as some lovely people who've written to me either when they heard we were making, or having seen, the show – I've got a few more tidbits.

Based on the conversations I've had with people after the show (sample: "So, did he really exist?" "Yes. Did I forget to say that several times in the show?" "No, but I thought that was you making it more clear that he didn't exist." "Surely that would be quite a weird way of saying that." "Yeah, but you are quite weird." "Good point. A Strongbow Dark Fruits please." "Strongbow Dark Fruits. Really?" "Don't judge me.") I thought it'd be good to talk a bit around the story, to weave some of these bits of tid into the script; to show how the show matches up with the true-life story as much as I know it.

This is not (repeat: not) the definitive Henry History, because as much as anything I'm not a historian and I don't have many primary sources. What I do have is a few family legends, local anecdotes, contemporary journo speculation, as well as bits of material we had to cut from the show because Alex and Eve (director and dramaturg) made me... sorry, I mean "to make the show better".

And so, here is all of that stuff, jostling around the main script like friendly little dolphins round a sailboat, in the form of footnotes, or feetnote, which – as we all know – is the plural of footnote*. Because I thought it might be cool.

I might be wrong, you might think this a very tiresome thing to do, but anyway I've done it now.

Seiriol Davies, *Woolwich, Friday 6th Jan 2017*

---

* – Yes, I know they're technically endnotes really, but I didn't think that was as pleasing a word as feetnote.

Devising the Show

We made the show through devising. For me, what that means is a process of us improvising, then me writing based on that, bringing what I'd wrote back to the room for us to read and then try it again, messing with it in an attempt to make it suck less, and so on back and forth.

"Us" in this instance was me and Matthew, then also Tom, and later Dylan, who are all tremendous men, and are moreover additionally men whom are happy to gad about in mime bloomers and belt out showtunes that are half (or quite often not at all) written.

Alex, the director, was in charge of everything that happened in the devising room, making sure we generated all the stuff I'd need to go off and write. Then, after we'd settled on a script, making sure that was as funny, sad, whatever, as we could make it. He'd also tell us vaguely where to stand, though that has never seemed a massive priority of his.

He's got this special technique where, when you do acting poorly, he shouts at you until you're doing it better. It's very modern and effective and I think is from Paris which explains a lot. In fact, the first thing he had us do on day one was the entire show, start to finish. I meekly told him we hadn't written it yet and he said he didn't care, we had to do it anyway. And then I've got this sort of redacted black memory hole for about two hours, during which I gather we made some useful discoveries.

We'd have a piano in the room, so that we could make up rough versions of the songs on the spot to see if the basic idea of them worked. This would save me sitting in my room smacking my hands away at my laptop like a Thunderbirds Jessica Fletcher on five espressos at 3am, hissing "THIS IS PERFECT GENIUS" through gritted teeth, and then playing it to everyone else at 10am and realising it was bad and cack.

We didn't really differentiate between 'songs' and 'scenes', because the way we work, a scene will always have the basic layer of what actually happens in the story (e.g. a man does an interview with the *Daily Mail* about his style choices) and a layer underneath which is a series of commands for the performer called the 'game' (every time the interviewer is looking up, the man lies, and every time the interviewer looks down, he tells the truth) which you don't talk about in the scene, but which ideally brings out some thematic aspect of what happens. Or makes it funnier, more tragic, odder.

Songs, we concluded, are sort of an enhanced version of this. With music, the genre you pick will send a number of subliminal messages to the person listening, as will tonality, timbre, pitch, speed and all that Year 9 music stuff. If a character's sad and they sing a happy song – BAM! Instant subtext. Contrasts you create between what a character's singing and how they're singing it can create really rich casseroles of sexy, herby meaning in people's heads.

Going into the whole process, I had a bunch of research I'd done in a slightly haphazard way over the several years I'd been a Henry fangirl. Breaking that down into story beats was an early task, and then playing about with those beats with improv, fleshing them out: finding the fun in them, the character growth, the thematic resonance and all that creamy goodness. Initially, there was a lot more of the actual research evident in the script: Henry would talk about various actual things he'd owned, or parts that he'd actually played, or actual amounts of money he'd pissed up the non-actual wall. However, these mostly fell away, as they would tend to slow things down, and just feel like "and now, another list of stuff Seiriol found on the internet."

Not that I wasn't livid that we kept cutting that material. "There's no *facts* left, Alex!" I would squeal; "*How* will people know that I spent literally *ages* looking them up?" But it's fine because now they said I could do this book, so bam.

Eve, the dramaturg, and I talked a lot about the research, the history and the character and so forth; she would also come in every so often to look at what we'd done and then we'd go for coffee and I'd wave my hands around and say the word "journey" a lot, and then she'd grin and say things of sageness.

'Dramaturg' is one of those words that can mean different things to different people, like 'pie'* or 'referendum'. The definition I go by, which I believe I nicked off Eve, is "someone who helps make the show more itself", i.e. more sad if it's supposed to be sad, more fast if it's supposed to be fast, more clearly about the international blackcurrant trade if it's supposed to be about the international blackcurrant trade.

I reckon it's important to put work in front of audiences regularly to test it while it's being developed: to see how it plays with different types of audience, and whether it's clear what's going on to any of them. With this sort of show, especially, given that we spend the whole time eyeballing the poor things and occasionally slightly sweating on them, it's doubly important.

We were lucky to be partnered early on with a venue: Ovalhouse Theatre, a supercool powerhouse of New Stuff, in S London, were very good to us from my first meeting with Rachel, then Director of Theatre there, where she was wearing adorable monster slippers and I was clutching some drawings of hats and the fourth cappuccino of the day. #thearts.

We then enpartnerised with Pontio, a stunning and vertiginous new arts centre in Bangor, N Wales, near where I (and Henry) grew up, meaning that we then had two places with very different audiences at which we could work on the show for a bit then do a Scratch performance. Rough showings are called 'Scratch' performances for some reason; I'm not sure why, or whether it's supposed to make you think '... and Sniff', but it does me.

So we'd show the rough bits we had to an audience, apologise profusely to them about how rough our bits were, get their feedback, then we could think about some changes for next time before starting the long process, of coffee-drinking and listening to inspirational Cher, known as fundraising. It's much easier to fill in endless application forms saying how great you are (or will be if you get the money) if you realise you're actually just in a montage sequence and that these long, dehydrated hours, spent squatting on a swivel chair in your favourite Marvel comics Tesco loungewear bouncing erratically as you type in time to "Save Up All Your Tears", will actually flit by in a few glamorous seconds when you look back on it later.

So it was like that, two weeks here, a week there, with big gaps inbetween when we scrabbled for money, that we made the show over like two years. Or more, counting the time before that Matthew and I spent doing cabarets, playing with embryonic ideas that would eventually become the show, with him with a big cardboard theatre on his head with a plastic baby and me dressed as a bishop.

So basically, to cut a long story long, it was long. I think that's good though, cos if nothing else it meant that by the time it finally opened, it was definitely the show we wanted to make. It would have greatly sucked if it had had to be rushed for some reason, gone off half-cocked, at a sad semi-spangle. I mean especially given that I've been banging on about this story since I was like twelve.

I would have been so annoying about that.

* – Do *not* try and fob me off with a casserole wearing a flaky hat, gastropub, so help me god.

PROLOGUE

*In which you're told pretty much the whole story upfront in case
you briefly lose consciousness for some reason later on.*

The BAND is in position at the piano. He is serious and professional, but has not necessarily seen this show before.

Enter Mr Alexander KEITH[1], a real actor. His every movement is practised and impressive. He would never dream of stealing the spotlight from HENRY, his benefactor. Ever.

KEITH opens the door to let HENRY in; KEITH directs the audience to start applauding.

HENRY[2] enters, and is surprised and delighted by the totally spontaneous applause. He is a fragile, gawky, optimistic, apologetic creature: a glassy man-child with matinée idol makeup and a fabulous frock. He looks like he taught himself to move by studying old paintings of sprites and nymphs. Instead of speaking, he sings in a gentle, mannered voice.

H: I am lonely,
    But I am rich.
    I am worried,
    But I'm a cross dresser.
    I am certain
    That I am fierce.
    I am an a-a-a-aristocrat.

KEITH cues a fulsome and triumphant chord from BAND at the piano, which surprises and delights HENRY, who had been slightly regretting starting this song. But he continues with élan.

H: Who is this man, standing in front of us as though it was
    no big deal?
    He can sing very well certainly, but what is his name
    we cannot see?
    Is his name Cuthbert?

He eyeballs someone in the front row, until they answer.

H: [*sotto*] No, no it's not Cuthbert.
    Is it Albert?

Gazes at another.

H: [*sotto*] It's not, no.
    Is it Henry?

Grins broadly at a third.

H: [*sotto*] It is, yeah.

He launches away into the next bit, with big hand gestures.

H: Henry, Henry Cyril,
          (Cyril is is his second name
          So he's Henry Cyril)
          Henry Cyril PAGET![3]
          And Paget is the third name,
          And it's the most important name
          Because it's the family name
          And family is

HKB: HISTORY!

HENRY is excited by the fact that he seems to have three voices and can self-harmonise.

He inadvertently twiddles a hand, and a musical swirl happens. He swirls again, pleased with his power. He swirls a third time and it becomes sad, and he realises that, yes, "sad" is correct.

H: Regrettably very little is known about my life. But I was an actual Edwardian noble, the Fifth Marquis of Anglesey, and one of the wealthiest men in the world![4] From a long line of other Marquises of Anglesey going back several years: war heroes[5] [*musical ripple*], landowners [*musical ripple*] and me [*a significant lack of ripple*].

He reckons this is fair enough, given how regrettable he is. Crikey.

H: Regrettably I may have led a regrettable life. Regrettably I died aged twenty-nine[6], penniless, in Monte Carlo.[7] Regrettably, I gutted the family chapel and built in its place a theatre[8] and then spent all of the family's money putting on plays with me in them.

K: And me...

H: And him! Regrettably after I died, my family annihilated every record of my existence, and burnt every trace of me: every photograph and document and letter in a fire.[9] [*enjoys being a fire with his hand*] [*realises not everyone can see him being a fire, so turns to face some different people to be a fire*]

H: So *hardly* any trace of me remains.

He finger-snaps. KEITH flies a book seamlessly into his hand. HENRY is surprised, in an impressed way, to find it in his hand.

H: I mean I do have this obituary that somebody actually wrote in real life. You can Google it if you want. Not now. "He is a melancholy and unneeded illustration that a man with the finest prospects may, by the wildest folly and extravagance, fouly miscarry in the advantage of... humanity, play away an uniterable life, and have lived in vain."[10] So there's that.

K: But...

H: But?

K: Don't worry, this will not be a difficult show. We don't mean to challenge you in any way.

H: [*gazing to a non-existent balcony*] No. I wish to "connect" with each and every one of you.

K: Myes.

'MAINSTREAM'

H: Now in the past I've been accused
            Of trying to be... clever,
            And I say "me? weird? and intellectually obscurantist?
HK: Never!"
H: I'm telling you I long to be obvious.
K: He's as easy to interpret as a dream.
H: That dream you have the night before you have to do
            something stressful,
            In which you have to do something stressful;
HK: That dream!

H: And in order to show that,
K: We've made this show that
H: Demonstrates I'm utterly
            Hopelessly devotedly

HK: Mainstream,
H: With this playlet
            I want everyone to know
            I'm going where I've always wanted to go:
HK: Mainstream entertainment,
H: It will be like I've made a cake and then put it inside your brain,
            And then you'll know what I know!

H: What do people want?
K: What do people want?
H: They want songs!
HK: Oh!
H: What do people want?
K: What do they want?
H: They want actors portraying more than one character, each with a different accent, because that is hard and clever. Ladies and gentlemen, mainstream actor Mr Alexander Keith!

KEITH takes centre stage.

K: 'O for a muse of fire, that would ascend. The brightest heaven of invention.'

A ta-dah on the piano. KEITH bows in response to some applause he assumes is happening.

K: Thank you. Yes it is I, Mr. Alexander Keith, a mainstream actor from the bustling West End of Victorian London.[11] Tonight, I hope to avail myself in the role of 'supporting performer', sharing what few meagre skills I have picked up over the many years treading the vulgar boards.

B: Dance break.

K: Oh!

KEITH does a frankly amazing dance which he never expected somebody would ask him to do.

HKB: Woo!
       Keith!
       Yeah! Oooooooh...

The dance ends and everyone enjoyed it very much.

K: And I also dance a little. This is

HK: Mainstream entertainment,
K: I will do my accents: 'stone the crows! Och, babby!'[12]
HK: This is mainstream entertainment,
H: So just sit back and think it's basically Downton Abbey!

HK: What do people want?
       What do people want?

H: They want events!
K: We've got nineteen of them!
H: Up to half of those are dramatic.

HK: What do people want?
           What do people want?
H: They want it to be a bit clever, like maybe the whole thing
           is a metaphor
           For the Bible, or
           The Greek myths, or
           The Mahabharata, or
           The Iraq War –
           Those are the main four –
           And this show has elements of all of them, probably,
           if you really really think about it.

They do for a bit.

HK: Audiences love
           To be flattered
K: But we'd never try to flatter you,
H: You're clearly way too intelligent.

HK: We really hate
           Going home from something,
           And you spend the whole way home
           Just trying to figure out what the hell it meant.

HKB: We wanna be like pistons
           Following the path of least resistance,
           Shooting from orifices of performance
           In a bee-line to your sensory organs.
           This is B B C One bliss,
           Keira Knightley could have been in this![13]

HK: This is mainstream entertainment,
K: I will use my acting chops to give you Happy, Normal, Sad.
HK: This is mainstream entertainment,
H: Ten minutes from the end it'll look like things are getting
           really bad,
HK: But then it gets better for a happy ending
HKB: Happy ending!

HK: Mainstream

B: Mainstream

HK: Entertainment,

H: As emotionally uncomplicated as Elton John's 'Your Song',

HK: This is mainstream

B: Mainstream

HK: Entertainment,
           And mainstream songs are abo-o-o-o-o-o-o-o-o-o-o-o-out
           This long.

This page intentionally left blank

SCENE 1
FONDLY TOUCHING CHILDHOOD MEM'RIES

In which boys will be boys, and also godlike overlords,
and our hero has a brief frisson of exhilarating, youthful, crippling doubt.

H: So here we are at Eton.[14] Oh!

HENRY is pleased by some lighting. KEITH prepares, in the manner of 'An Actor Prepares'.

H: Eton School College for Posh Boys of the Gentry, a place where all your nightmares come true: it's very character building.

HENRY polishes his boot. KEITH comes in as Cameron, who trots around like he's doing dressage and speaks in little machine gun volleys not literally.

K: Good morning Paget I hate you.

Slaps HENRY from the opposite end of the room which, after a slight delay, sends him flying.

H: Oh, Cameron, my bunk-mate, I didn't see you there in this room we share here at Eton.[15]

K: What are you doing down there on the floor you little oik?

H: I'm just polishing my boots for the Eton military parade.[16] Oh but look at your boots – they are frankly superduposly shiny and put mine to shiny shame! And those feathers on your helmet. Will you please help me be just like you?

K: Of course, we're all friends here at Eton. You there, play the piano, I'm going to do a song.

'BOOTS AND FEATHERS'

K: Now
        Let me explain to you, old pal, the
        Eton[17] fagging[18] way: the boys like
        You give older boys like me
        A "hand" about their day. You'll be my
        Catamite, my storage rack,
        My toilet warmer too, so that my
        Chilly old Napoleon can
        Meet his warmer loo. Pun!
H: Hahaha.
K: However freezing cold becomes the weather
        Because, old chum: we're all in this together[19]

H:　　Gosh Cameron, that's a very effective slogan Cameron!

K:　　Yes. Now shut up your arse so I can tell you some more stuff. You see it's

K:　　Just way of letting children
　　　　Play at being slaves, and it's
　　　　Clear to see in the long run all the
　　　　Lives the system saves; because it's
　　　　Not just slaves we play at being, it's
　　　　Also being GOD. It'll be so
　　　　Useful in ten years or so when you're
　　　　Out there on your tod
　　　　Among so many strange and foreign faces;
　　　　Don't be afraid, just give a little tug on your
　　　　Rule Britannia laces

HK:　　Wearing:

KEITH does a dainty little lovely dance with his butchly pointy boot-feet.

HKB:　　Boots, boots, boots, boots
　　　　Boots, boots, boots and feathers,
　　　　Boots, boots, lovely shiny boots,
　　　　Very nice shiny boots and lovely feathers.
　　　　Oh we British are so divine
　　　　Just because we're so masculine,

K:　　/ Watch me go, I'll surely knock 'em dead
　　　　With feathers on my head!

HB:　　/ Watch him go, he'll surely knock 'em dead
　　　　With feathers on his head!

H:　　Gadzooks Cameron, that is the best song ever![20]

K:　　I know. You see, there are so many places where the British Empire's presence has ensured that peace and order will abide for ever more: West Africa, Afghanistan, Palestine, Iraq, all fixed. You're welcome. You see history will judge us, and it will judge us well. Because history is written by the winners. And it is also won by the winners. And we are the winners.

H:　　Oh my gosh!
　　　　You are such a manly cove, with
　　　　Such a thrusting crutch, let me
　　　　Be your empty vessel, I want to

Learn to be so... butch. Just like
Wellington, and Nelson, and his
Hardy-kissing ilk, a
Man is never prouder than in
Pantaloons of silk.
With rigid seams just here where I am lumpy,
Which are irritating and make me sort of perma-grumpy,
they're awful!

K: Quite right, nobody ever died because an Englishman was slightly grumpy. As my old Latin and Eugenics master, Major Rod McDominator, used to say: "Show me a man who's slightly miffed, and he will conquer the world very swift". And that's obviously true.

H: Yes! It rhymes!

K: Exactly.

H: My mamma, who, as you know, died when I was very young[21], leaving me in the loving arms of my cold and distant father[22], used to say 'be yourself'.[23]

K: BE YOURSELF? *Whom* do you think you are? *Whym* are you here? *Howm* do you think this works? You're an aristocrat Paget: not technically a person. You're an icon, a symbol, connected to a whole that is far far bigger, and old, and weird, and flaggy.

H: And great!

K: Where you walk, the Empire walks. If you wave a sabre at some cannibals, it's not you waving a sabre: it's the Empire.

H: If I wear hot pants and a Geisha mask, the Empire wears hotpants and a Geisha mask!

K: Well I never, what a silly clot you are. Have up Paget, you've dampened my spirits being such a spoddy malco. Why don't you sing the Eton School College for Posh Boys of the Gentry School Song? That never fails to rouse me.

HENRY boy sopranos. It is v Carols From King's.

H: E-ton E-ton, pull up a peasant to put your feet on,
Look into the future, see your place in it.
K: Spo-iler a-lert: it is at the to-op.
H: Fuck the poor!

All are upstanding. Or at least ought to be and, if not, can be glared at for not being.

HKB: I want to
Join the greatest chain and be its
Shiniest little link, I want to
Be a part of painting all the
World a lovely pink. Let us
Strap into our cos-tumes and a
Marching marching go

B: *Where the streets are paved with plebs.*

HKB: We are not men, we're
Supermen, and we'll
Let those foreigns know

K: *(Silly foreigns).*

HKB: With nothing but natural su-periori-ty.

B: *We also have guns.*

H: But ma-in-ly-y natural
Su-pe/ri-ori-ty

KB: / Superiority:

K: *We are the best.*

HK: Check out our...

They go into the dance again, and HENRY tries to join in.

HKB: Boots, boots, boots, boots
Boots, boots, boots and feathers,
Boots, boots, lovely shiny boots,
Very nice shiny boots and lovely feathers.
Oh we British are so divine
Just because we're so masculine –

K: No! Whenever you sing it you always make it sound so gay, which in this time period means 'happy'. It's really a very serious song. Let's do it again, but this time think butch thoughts. Think about men in moustaches pummeling each other hard, eyes wide with admiration. A-five, six, seven, eight!

They do it again but faster and more butcher. HENRY is struggling.

HKB: Boots, boots, boots, boots
Boots, boots, boots and feathers,
Boots, boots, lovely shiny boots,
Very nice shiny boots and lovely feathers.

	Oh we British are so divine
	Just because we're so masculine,
K:	/ Watch me go, I'll surely knock 'em dead
	With feathers on my –
HB:	/ Watch him go, he'll surely knock 'em dead
	With feathers on his –

K: No!

HENRY is frozen in place, with mime head-dress and hips still jiggling to the rhythm.

K: What's the point in explaining anything to you? You're nothing but a silly frilly frolly frolly frilly frilly frop. Good day I hate you.

He leaves, slamming the door in HENRY's face. A second later, HENRY goes flying.

H: Frilly frop!
          Frolly frilly? Fie!
          I am indeed a silly frilly frolly frolly frilly frilly frop like he said.
          Nothing but a froofy, frill-conceived, flip and froleaginous frool
          Fridly frollicking in my own frill-deserved fropulence,
          Oh my head!
          The fruity fladvice and flat-out bad frights
          A-flaps in my brain, a-driving me frinsane!
          What will I doooo?
          I give up.

He falls to ground.

H: But wait! What is that a-coming through the wall, as though arriving in a ghostly way from the future, or space...

KEITH wafts in through a curtain.

K: Do not fret young Henery, for we are two ghosts from the future or space.[24] I am the first ghost and this is my friend, another ghost...

Indicates BAND, who is another ghost.

B: Hello, I am also a ghost.

HENRY screams.

K: And we are here to deliver you...

KB: A prophecy-yyyyyyyyooooOOOOH!

BAND goes a bit OTT on the old spooky woos; KEITH steadies him with 'steady on now' woahs.

'THE PROPHECY'[25]

KB: Stupid-looking crying child!
H: Sob.
KB: Stupid-looking crying child.
H: Sniff.
KB: Stop crying.
H: Sniff sob.
KB: Stop-cry-ing!
H: Waaaaaaaaaaaaaaaaaaa-aaaaaa-aaaaaail!
KB: Okay, multitask,
            And listen.

KB: Henry Cyril,
            We are the ghosts of prophecy.
            Prophecy!
            Henry Cyril, hail to thee!
            The Marquis of Anglesey thou shalt be
            Hereafter!
H: Obviously,
            I mean, it's hereditary.
K: Is it?
KB: You are bo-orn with ex-pec-tations-great;
            Way more than your ass-hat classmates,
B: Way more!
K: Flippin' cor,
KB: Blimey one day they'll regret it [*gasp!*]

K: No presh, but we expect
B: Very big things from you.
K: No presh,
B: Huge,
K: No presh,
B: Huge,

K: No presh

B: Absolutely

KB: Enormous.
         Yes!
         Huge things, huge things,
         I mean seriously,

They layer, and it starts to become a madrigal.

B: / Huge things, huge things,
         I mean seriously,
         // Huge things, huge things,
         I mean seriously,
         Huge things, huge things,
         I mean serious pressure!

K: / No presh, no presh, no presh,
         No presh, no presh, no presh,
         // No presh, no presh, no presh,
         No presh, no presh, no presh, no
         Presh, no presh, no presh no pressure!

H: // Can you be a bit more specific?
         You're not being very specific.
         I would like you to be a bit more specific in this song that you're...

HENRY is knocked backwards by the force of how little pressure there is.

K: Anyway

B: Hope that helps,

KB: End of prophecy
         Bye bye!

The ghosts hide behind the piano. HENRY puts his hand up patiently like in school.

They come back awkwardly.

B: Um, yes?

H: So, was there some actual advice?

B: Oh.

K: Right.

B: Oh I know this one... be yourself!

H: Be my*self?*

K: Be yourself!

H: Be *my*self?

B: *Be* yourself.

K: Be it.

H: Be... my... self –

B: Whatcha wanna be, now do it!

K: Just be yourself, get to it

KB: NOW!

HENRY tries to do as he's told and be himself. But he doesn't really know what it means.

H: Look at that butterfly...

KB: Yeah!

H: I will wear...

KB: Yeah?

H: Lovely, lovely dresses![26]

KB: Yeah! What?

H: Mhm.

B: Whatever!

H: Lovely dresses!

K: Yeah!

KB: Good luck with that!

The ghosts high-five; their hands pass through each other. They, pleased, recall they are ghosts.

KB: Ghosts!

They spookily vanish, and BAND immediately reappears to play the piano.

HENRY goes into beautiful mode, with beautiful lighting, serving pure Maurice Binder Bond film opening titles slash Julianna Margulies in promotional material for The Good Wife realness.

KEITH slinks behind him like a narrating panther.

K: And so the ghosts gazed upon young Henery, and they saw that their prophecy had clearly found purchase in the young boy's mind, for he had changed out of his drab Eton School College for Posh Boys of the Gentry smock and velvet striding-johns and was being himself in a very spangly dress. And the dress was silvery-bluey, and it was sequins, and it shone like the very actual moon itself. And the dress was called...

H: Hope?

/ Be Myself!
KB: / Be Yourself!

A moment of tacet slash pause.[27]

SCENE 2
A TYPICAL, ENTRY-LEVEL COURTSHIP

*In which our hero meets a woman, and discovers
what goes together with love like a horse and carriage: a horse.*

H: And so, at the age of twenty-three, what I did was I got engaged – I know!

Enter KEITH as Lilian, with mime bustle. There is much giddy excitement between them.

H: To the most beautiful girl in the world: Lilian Florence Maud Chetwynd. She had such long, gold Titian hair. Do not worry if you do not know who Titian is – just look him up.[28] Her mother before her was also a beauty, but she had an affair with a man in a shop so we do not talk about her.[29] It was assumed that Lilian would inherit her mother's weak character and so it was imperative that she marry as quickly as possible the man who would be the least trouble...

HENRY proudly identifies himself as that man. KEITH glides in comme costume drama avec high-quality mimed bustle acting. They are awkward and thrilled; she is Margery Tyrell sultry.

K: Hello cousin.

H: Which is normal in this time period.[30] Hello.

K: "Shall I come in?"[31]

She does quotation marks with her fingers. She is offering him a game, and he joins in quickly.

H: Oh, yes. "Come in". Nice bustle.

K: "Thank you". As you know, we are both young and have large trusts of money due to us.

H: "Yes."

K: And as you also know, we can only unlock that money if we are to "marry"... someone, in the normal way.

H: Ah. [*crosses the stage to make the scene more realistic*] "Yes."

K: Good. So we have "an understandiiiiiiing?"

H: "Yeah".

Beat.

H: "Shall we have some tea?"

K: Oh yes, that would be normal. "Yes."

He bounds over to a mime bell-pull.

H: Dingaling... "It'll be up in a minute."

KEITH takes the opportunity to be extra sultry and advance on him with a fan.

H: Oh look here it is.

A mime tea trolley arrives, just in time – that was getting weird!

K: How normal. "Shall I be mother?"

H: URK! Oh, with the tea?

K: Yes with the tea, yes.

H: And then later...

K: Oh!

H: Oh!

K: Perhaps actually.

To break the tension, she pours the mime tea. He enjoys doing sound effects – they're working well as a team. They drink. She pushes the trolley away. It crashes into the audience. They apologise.

K: "So."

H: So.

K: So. "Shall we get engaged now?"

H: Oh, yes.

KEITH presents her hand to be taken. HENRY doesn't understand and happily copies what she's doing and puts his hand out because she looks fetch doing it. She puts hers under his and he puts his under hers in a sort of reverse patty-cake, him giggling and her manhandling him to his knee. They realise they are in exactly the correct position for getting engaged in.

K: Oh! what a surprise.

H: Will you... marry me?

K: Oh, yes.

H: Yay!

They shake hands vigorously.

K: Excellent, I think we did that very well.

A pause.

H: Now, it is nearly four o' clock, shall we gather round the piano and sing songs of love?

K: Yes, that sounds like exactly the sort of thing we'd do.

KEITH goes over to the real piano, expecting that to be the piano in question. But no! HENRY goes over to a mime piano, opens the lid and plays a note, which BAND dubs. Everyone is impressed.

HENRY is like no big deal and plays the intro on his mime piano. It is pure stage magic.

'THIS IS WHAT IT LOOKS LIKE'[32]

H: There is a strange idea
That "art" is a compliment,
That the word "art" is a compliment.
It's not, it's just a type of thing,
A category like bacteria or knitwear.

K: There is a strange idea
That love is an accomplishment,
That "being in love" is an accomplishment,
It's not, it's just something you decide to do
And then act accordingly and then that's it, there.

HENRY gets serious on his mime piano.

H: If I dress like a ho-o-orse
And do the sound of a horse, and say 'hey I'm a horse',
I'd be a horse, right?
If I'm convincingly dressed like a horse!

K: If I marry you of co-o-ourse
It means I "love you", doesn't it?

H: Think so.

K: 'Cos that's what people doing love do,
They say 'hey look I'm going to marry you'.

H: Then they get married in an irreverent traditional-slash-not-traditional ceremony
That really reflects them as people

HENRY starts wandering around.

H: And occasionally it turns out that they are more traditional than you think
Which gives their guests an opportunity to be uppity about that sort of thing
And then they stand next to each other and try not to dress too similarly
Because that would make them insufferable
And they try to tell funny stories of stuff that happened to them
And it becomes weirdly competitive
Because each of them is used to telling this story when there was just one of them
But now there's two of them which is literally twice as many

K: Which means they have to share...

H: Yeah! And people are like 'this is actually all getting a bit stressful
But I expect they'll iron it out, those two
Because they're young'... ish, I mean early thirties – that *is* still young right?
And they're married so they must need each other...
Need
Open brackets wobbly line over straight horizontal line meaning approximately equal to[33]

HK: Love.

H: Close brackets. 'Cos

HK: This is what it looks like
To feel what we should feel,
This is what it looks like,
This is what it looks like
To be real people.

K: There is a strange idea
That judging a book by its cover,

H: That is, assessing the nature of a book by
Consulting the visual information on the cover,

K: Is something you should never do...

H: And I think that that's ridiculous and misunderstands the
Basic technical function of a book's cover.

HENRY finds another mime piano over here, plays the riff and dismisseth it immediately.

K: There is a strange idea
That clothes maketh the man,

H: Or in your case, I suppose, "woman",

HK: But it's not quite that simple, there's also
Parties.

H: And if you have a pa-a-a-rty,
And invited everyone you knew,
You would see that the biggest gift would be from me.[34]

K: This one?

H: No, the one behind it...

K: But it's huge!

LILIAN opens a vast and beautiful invisible present. Inside is napkin rings (also invisible).

H: And inside would be

HK: Napkin rings!

H: 'Cos that's what you need, right?
Really good napkin rings for a dinner party,
'Cos that's what dinner parties are about
Control, setting, the theatre of mystique...

K: I love them!

H: But...

K: I *love* them.
Because

HK: This is what it looks like
To have a fancy meal,
This is what it looks like,
This is what it looks like
To be real people

K: And singing a song like this is what it sounds like
To feel.

H: It sounds like you feel a great deal!

B: *Feel a great deal!*

K: Why thank you.

H: So is this the sort of level
Of convihihincingness we'll need to be at
To pass as a real couple?

K: You nailed it!

B: *You nailed it!*

H: You're too kind!
But what if they don't believe us?
What if we make a mistake?

K: Then we'll do it all so big they'll know we're
Definitely not fake, we'll give 'em

HK: More face more face more aristocrat face
And walk and walk and walk, swishy lace,
We know what they expect and we will do it just right,
A couple of normal people,
Normal people,

K: / Normal people –

H: / Normalpeoplevestites![35]
We'll make them gag on realness[36]

K: And I'll never have to touch your penis, right?

H: Nope!

HK: So I will

H: Wear the kind of thing I'd wear

K: I'll kiss the way a real person would kiss,

HK: I'll pick my skirts up thusly
And I'll walk like this

H: And when they see us walking by

HK: In our camouflage doing good badinage
'Ha ha ha!'

H: They won't think 'who are they they're weird?'

K: They'll think: 'There's Lilian and her husband who's a

HK: Fine – up – stand – ing

H: HORSE!'
Because I will be dressed as a horse.
Phrrrh!
Or man, I can do man, that's fine. 'Cos...

HK: This is what it looks like
To feel, to feel, to feel

H: Loveloveloveloveelove quintuple.

K: Times five as much

HK: This is what it looks like,
This is what we look like
As a couple
Of real people.

Awkward pause as we look at them as a couple. They are straining
from each other while clasped in a grinning embrace.

H: Apparently things didn't turn out that well. Allegedly
I treated Lilian quite badly. We were the perfect couple: had
breakfast, wore hats, went to Paris. Apparently one day I saw
Lilian looking in a jewellery shop window.[37]

K: [*sotto*] Oh, that's nice isn't it?

H: And I went in the shop.

K: [*sotto*] Henry, what are you doing?

H: And I bought the entire shop...

K: [*sotto*] Henry, nooo!

H: ... and I put the entire shop on her and made her wear it
all at the same time. Allegedly at bedtime I made her take off all
her clothes (until she was naked), and then in lieu of making "love"
in the conventional manner, I put diamonds all over her body.[38]

They are in separate mime tableaux because they are troubled as a
couple. HENRY is not looking at KEITH, who is bent over backwards
uncomfortably in a strained representation of having jewels put on his
naked body.

H: Amazing, Amazing,
This is our life.
Look at her, so normal,
My hyper-realistic wife

K: Henry, I'm leaving you.[39]

He slowly turns to her.

H: That is... amazing, so realistic!

K: No really, Henry...

H: I know, so exactly what a real woman would do in this situation.

K: Henry, this is an event. I am a real woman, and I've fallen in love.

H: Don't you mean "love"?

K: I want a divorce.

H: Then I will be... the perfect divorcee.

K: Goodbye Henry.

She leaves, having a bit of trouble with bustle admin trying to get through a narrow mime doorway.

H: Amazing, Amazing,
My hyper-realistic wife.

This page intentionally left blank

SCENE 3
THE MARQUISING

In which roughly three of the aforementioned "dramatic events" occur just bam bam bam like that in a row.

H: And then my father died.[40]

KB: The Marquis of Anglesey thou shalt be hereafter!

H: The Prophecy, of courseness!

B: Told you.

H: But what do I do?

KEITH flies in with a feathered helmet of glory. HENRY, petrified, is crowned Marquis of All Anglesey.

KB: Huge things, huge things,
           Huge things, huge things,

H: This is what it looks like to be a Ma / ar-

KB: / Ma-a-ar

H: Quis!

HENRY sits on a pillar slash throne, trying to serve 'Marquis' realness.

'HE IS A GOOD MARQUIS'

H: So now we are a Marquis,
           But what are a Marquis for?
           I mean we've got all these rural subjects now
           Who are predominantly poor...
           What can we give them?

K: Money?

B: Cash?

K: Money.

H: Ngh. What can we give them?
           The most precious thing we have:
           Art!

           We will put on a play, but what is the perfect
           Play for them to see?
           My name is Henery

KB: Henery

HKB: The Fifth

H: Marquis of Anglesey;
           Is there a play called Henery the Marquis?

K: No.

H: Nergh. Is there a play called Henery the like Fi-ifth?[41]

KB: Yes!

H: Oh right fine we'll do that one then!
           We'll need an orchestra!

B: I'm available!

H: Actors![42]

K: Enter: me!

H: Financial backing.

KB: You're very rich!

K: And we'll need a theatre.

H: Awww, we don't have one of those!

B: But chaps, we could pray for a theatre – in the old Paget family chapel.

HENRY has a brilliant idea.

H: Gut the family chapel!

KB: Gut it!

H: And build in its place a theatre,
           In egg-shell blue[43] I think.

K: [*taking notes*] Yes, egg-shell blue!

H: Light a trail of flaming torches
           Right to the door of the theatre
           So all the Angleseysyans
           Will know which way to flock to[44]
           When they come to see the

KEITH becomes a succession of artisans with whom HENRY shakes hands. In the background we assume there are hundreds of servants endlessly billowing tablecloths and sawing things and raising poles.

H: / Play, the play, the play, it's on
           Today, by which I mean tonight, what will they
           Say? What will they say when they have
           Seen me in the play

K: / Play, the play, the play, the
           Play, the play, the play, it's on
           Tonight, by which I mean tonight, what will they
           Say when they have seen me in the
           Play?

H: In my lovely sapphire costume[45]
           And my sword that's basically just one long
           Swarovski crystal![46]

K: Bling!

B: Bling!

K: Bling!

B: Ding!

K: Theatre construction is complete![47]
H: The play's the thing you'll see to make my
         Subjects sing:
B: 'The play, the play, the play'
         They'll say

H: 'He is a good Marquis!'
K: So good.
H: 'He's such a good Marquis!'
K: He pays well.
H: 'Only he could give us this!'
K: Plus it's good exposure.
H: 'He's such a good Marquis!'
         Now open up the doors and
HK: Let them...
         IN!
K: Open box office! Go front of house! Sell those
         programmes!
H: Let them IN!

They run out onstage w/ great excitement... then stop w/ the opposite
of great excitement.

SCENE 4
UNTO THE PEOPLE

In which our hero receives life advice from an actor.

H: Where is everybody?

KEITH shrugs.

H: Regrettably, nobody turned up to my first production.[48] But other than that, it was very well-received.

K: It was very good.

H: See!

K: But Henery... If I may just slip my little multi award-nominated oar into the proceedings. If you ask me, the problem here was all actually in the marketing.

H: Marquissing?

K: Yes! I mean lighting flaming torches to the door of the theatre is lovely, but it's a bit... 'concept' isn't it? To get people to come see a play, you need to use things that definitely always work, like flyers.[49]

H: Right.

K: And we can't just be putting on the play here in our lovely theatre and expect a big turnout, oh jolly giggles no. After all, if the mountain won't come to Mohammed...

HENRY looks blankly.

K: If the mountain won't come to Mo-*Henry*...

HENRY looks blankly. Addresses a nearby audient.

H: [*sotto*] I think he's talking to you.

K: No. If the audience won't come to MoHenry...

H: Then Mo-Henry will... cry?

K: No.

H: No, obviously not, no.

K: ... If the audience won't come to MoHenry, then MoHenry must go to the audience!

H: Great! Am I called MoHenry now?

K: No.

H: Checking!

K: It's time to do one of the most exciting things of an actor's life.

H: Yes!

K: Provincial touring!

H: Proventa toora!

K: So[50] we vagabond muffins lash our knapsacks to our knaps and set off to take the show...

HK: On the road!![51]

KEITH holds up a placard saying 'APPLAUSE', and the audience does that, totally willingly.

KEITH turns the card over, and on the other side it says 'RIOTOUS APPLAUSE'. Everyone goes literally wild.

'PLEASE EVERYBODY (THE TOURING SONG)'

The three of them get behind the piano as though it were a jolly car. BAND is driving. HENRY honks a horn on the dashboard, and KEITH provides the honking sound with aplomb.

HKB: Travelling along on a really nice day,
Don't you just love a-doing a touring play?
H: I do like costumes
K: I love collaboration
H: I like big lights
B: Service stations!
K: The director giving me precise direction,
Then I just do something that feels right!
H: It's about connection!

HKB: Theatre's a temple
With every soul
Gathering together
With the same goal:
H: To look at me,
K: To look at me,

H: To look at me,
K: To look at me,
HK: I mean 'art'.

HKB: We're loose from our tether,
We're travelling together
To put on a show that
Everyone will love!

B: Ladies and gentlemen, we present Oscar Wilde's *An Ideal Husband*,[52]
Starring the Marquis of Anglesey as the ideal husband,
And Mr Alexander Keith as a non-ideal husband.

KEITH and HENRY create a tableau of two men about to have a good and witty chat with moustaches. As in they're chatting while having moustaches on, not as in they're talking to the moustaches, as that would be a bit much even for the iconoclastic Wilde.

HKB: Cur-tain up!

Blackout.

Lights back up on an image of them backstage. KEITH holds up a placard that reads 'RESPECTFUL APPLAUSE'. The three of them accept the audience's golf clapping with grace.

K: How do you think it went?
H: How d'you think it went?
B: How d'you think it went?
HB: You first.
K: Okay, I think it's the
First week, I think we're all still tired from
Rehearsal, but other than that it went well!
HB: It went well, it went well!
HKB: I think they liked it.
H: That lady with the notepad was a bit distracting,
I think I stared at her in basically all of my acting
K: Was there something just a little unexciting?
H: Even with the haze effects and all that lighting?
K: But trying to second guess the audience is tough.
H: Maybe it just wasn't fabulous enough...
HKB: Oh well.
You can't please everybody all the time.

They get back in the car slash tour van I mean it's the piano but just go with it. HENRY honks the horn again, but KEITH's sound effect is delayed.

HKB: Travelling along on a pretty nice day,
          Don't you just love a-doing a touring play
K: I like the smell of the stage and the backdrop –
H: And the sky!
B: I love being paid to make strangers cry.
K: The ducking and diving, the rolling with punches,

HENRY winds down his window and sticks his head out, tongue lolling like a dog.

H: The feeling aliveing!
B: Unionised lunches!
K: We're riffing some changes,
H: Living on the edge!
K: Responding to feedback!
B: I just drove in a hedge!

They crash in a hedge, because HENRY and KEITH were agreeing with each other really hard right in front of BAND's face.

HK: Never mind! Because we're
HKB: Light as a feather,
          We're travelling together
          To put on a show that
          Everyone will love.

B: We present a searing adaptation of Oscar Wilde's masterpiece:
          'An Eye dot Deal forward slash Husb AND?'
          Starring Mr Alexander Keith as the ideal husband,
          And the Marquis of Anglesey as Crystal, the family dog.[53]

HKB: Cur-tain up!

KEITH is the same as in the last tableau, but HENRY is now an enthusiastic pooch. Awuff!

Blackout.

Lights up. KEITH holds a 'THE SOUND OF ONE PERSON CLAPPING' placard, until someone does. The three of them point that person out clearly to make sure nobody else claps as well.

H: How do you think it went?

K: How d'you think it went?

B: How d'you think it went?

HK: You first.

B: Okay, I think it's like
        Week five, and we're all feeling some
        Fatigue now, but accounting for that

K: It went well!

HB: It went well, it went well!

HKB: No it was good I thought.

K: I'm not sure they really "got" it...

H: You're right, more glitter, I will enter by rocket,
        And ten more mirrorballs, I want total immersion,
        And a sub-plot about a butterfly who thinks he's a person,[54]
        No sleep tonight, they've gotta love our guts!

K: Scripts out people, 'cos we're making some cuts,

HKB: 'Cos you should please everybody
        All the time.

The car is where they are, encore. HENRY honks again, but KEITH just can't any more, and just goes 'uuuuuuugh'.

HKB: Travelling along on a ... day
        Don't you just love a-doing a touring play?

H: I love the camaraderie!

HENRY beams at his pals, whose pallishness is not currently evident. A bit of a pause.

K: I love it when people actually hit their cues.

B: [*mocking him*] "I love it when people actually hit their cues."

K: Excuse me, I'm right here.

B: [*this is his line*] 'I love the pub'.

K: *Thank you.*
    Encore de silence.

B: This used to be my hobby.
    Silencio.

B: I don't have a hobby any more.
    El tacet.

H: And when the audience comes in
        And they don't know what to expect...

K: And then they see you.

	And if they like you, you win.
H:	And if they don't like you?
K:	*THEY WIN.*
	And... thus... we're

HKB:	Working together
	Hell for leather
	To put on a show
	That they have got to love!

B:	Ladies and gentlemen, we present:
	'An Ideal Dog'.
	A tone poem in seventeen identical stanzas,
	Starring Mr Alexander Keith as the emotional backdrop,
	And the Marquis of Anglesey in the key and titular role of Crystal.

HENRY is in a pose that is equal parts the creative destruction god Shiva and the symbol of the former artist formerly known as Prince. But is still also a dog. Ruff!

HKB:	Cur-tain up!

Blackout.

Lights back up on an image of them backstage. KEITH holds up a placard that reads 'THE SOUND OF ABSENCE'.

B:	How do you think it went?
K:	How d'you *think* it went?
H:	How d'you think it went?
KB:	You first.
H:	Okay, well... some of them stayed, which I thought was interesting, And of course we're near the end of the tour now, so we're all really tired, but...
K:	That was disgusting.
B:	Awful.
H:	Really?
K:	Oh not us, dear boy!
B:	We were quite fine.
K:	There's only so much you can do to *pander to an audience.*
B:	Quite right, I think Some people just find non-clappy forms Of emotional release, DON'T THEY!

They posture around at the audience, who are clearly in their bad books.

K: And even then, I'd rather die than make
          A non-Marmite piece.

KB: I really think tonight the fault was theirs.

H: And I like that bit with the lighty-up stairs.

K: But it's not our place to give an easy laff
          You've got to separate the wheat from the chaff,

HKB: 'Cos you can't please everybody
          All the time.

H: Whatcha say?

HKB: You can't please everybody,

B: And maybe you shouldn't please anybody,

HKB: You can't please everybody
          All the time.

K: And that's fine.

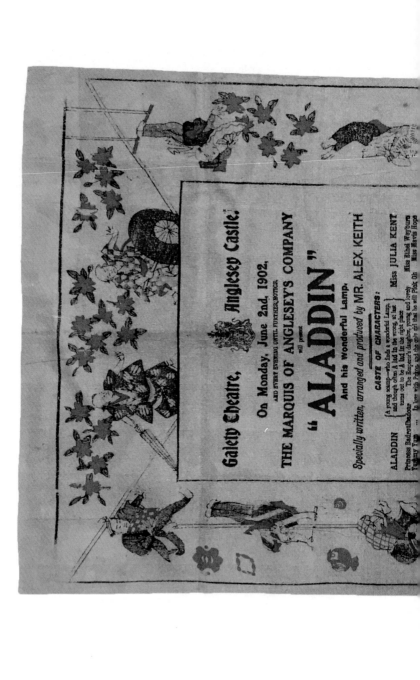

Gaiety Theatre, Anglesey Castle.

On Monday, June 2nd, 1902,

AND EVERY EVENING UNTIL FURTHER NOTICE.

THE MARQUIS OF ANGLESEY'S COMPANY

will present

"ALADDIN"

And his Wonderful Lamp.

Specially written, arranged and produced by MR. ALEX. KEITH

CASTE OF CHARACTERS:

ALADDIN {A young scamp—who finds a wonderful Lamp, and though often A lad in the wrong, at last turns out to be A lad in the right place. ... Miss JULIA KENT

Princess Badroulbadour   The Emperor's daughter, young, and lovely ... Miss Ethel Weyburn

Tushy Yum ...   In love with Pabro and the poor girl that he will Pink Oh ... Miss Mavis Hope

supposed to have dished out the pantomime

	Two Chung Bobbies, who Rob in and out yet hasn't a Bob between them	{ Mr. Charles R. Wrighton Mr. W. H. Murphy
Rusham }		
Pusham }		
Abenaxaar	A Magician, an important Character, though he hasn't one	Mr. ALEX KEITH
She-Sang	...	Miss Claudi Hope
Ho-Sang	Chinese Ladies	Miss Josephine Collier
Sing-Song		Miss Evelyn Hope
Wun-Hi	...	Mr. Gerald Alexander
Win-Jung	Oddments (from the Potteries)	Mr. Frank Hilton
La-di-da		Miss Blanche Trevalyon
Pomme-de-Terre }		Miss Olive Clowes
Ping-Pong }	Vampfelish }	Miss Frances Arnold

and

Prince Pekoe (The Vizier's Son — on Royalty on) **MARQUIS OF ANGLESEY**
(Funny Yum, who is his guiding Star)

SYNOPSIS OF SCENERY:

Scene 1—The Market Place, Pekin. Scene 2—On the road to the Cave. Scene 3—Interior of the Cave. Instantaneous Change to Scene 4—The Cave of Jewels.

INTERVAL OF TEN MINUTES.

Scene 5—Widow Twankey's Kitchen. Scene 8—Widow Twankey's Bedroom.
Scene 7—Corridor in the Emperor's Palace. Scene 8—The Magic Palace.
Scene 9—Cloudland. Scene 10—Abanazar's Palace. Scene 11—Aladdin's Palace.

In Scene 4 will be introduced

The Butterfly Dance, by The Marquis of Anglesey

Musical Director	{ Mr. FRANCIS KNOWLES
For Mr. ALEX KEITH	{ Mr. HORACE WILTON
Assistant Stage Manager	

New and Magnificent Costumes by Messrs. Morris Angel & Sons, London, and Messrs. W. Clarkson, London; Marquis of Anglesey's Special Dresses by Messrs. Buckinshaw, Liverpool;
Wigs by Clarkson. Morris Angel & Sons, London and Mons. Landolff, Paris.

EVERY EVENING AT 7.45.   CARRIAGES AT 11.

Jarvis & Foster, London, Yorks, Bristol

SCENE 5
BIG IN GERMANY

In which our brave lads attempt to beat David Hasselhoff to being the biggest thing to hit Germany since World War 2, before either of those things even happened.

A pause occurs of longness. HENRY gets out of the car with saddity.

H: Yes, and but you say that... and but it still... does not *feel* great.

K: Henery.

H: What?

K: Here we are back at your palace. Put down your heavy load, order us a baguette – or whatever you have in – and come, list.

HENRY comes and lists, which also means 'to lean'. It is one of the clever moments of humour.

K: I know first hand how difficult it is to be an actor. I know it's hard to believe, but even I have been slow-clapped offstage when I gave my Titus Andronicus. I have performed to smaller and less interested houses even than this one, and did it upset me? Yes, a little. But! the joke's on them! For I am an actor, and if there's one thing actors are good at, it's ignoring rejection.

H: I noticed that!

K: Henery! If a tree falls in the forest, and there's no one there to hear it, does it still make a sound?

HENRY looks blank. KEITH decides to be less metaphorical.

K: If a *man* is fabulous in a theatre, and there's no one there to see it, is he still fabulous?

H: [*absolutely immediately*] Yes. [*massive mental thunderstrike*] Oh my gosh...

K: If you speak with honesty and authenticity, everyone will understand you. To be the best version of one's self, an actor must be naked on the stage [*HENRY is excited*] Not literally. [*HENRY is disappointed*] And to learn this craft you must go to the place where Truth rules above all. We must go to that most romantic of all countries, with the most sensual of all languages and sonorous of all accents: Germany. A good friend of mine, Lord Berners, a prominent aesthete[55] – i.e. someone who is into this kind of thing – lives in Dresden, and he says it really is a hotbed of stuff at the moment. And so we to Germany.

They become in Dresden.

HK: Oh.

H: Here we are in Dresden. It really is a beautiful city, I do hope that nothing awful ever happens to it. But I must away to prepare, for tonight I will be performing my 'Electric Butterfly Dance' in a notorious German musikhalle, or music hall.

HENRY goes to the back of the stage for a bit. BAND does oom-pah music.

K: Look at this music hall! It's got everything: curtains, drapes, a ceiling – the lot. Now in this scene, I shall be playing my good friend Lord Berners. In fact oh look here he is: Hello Lord Berners!

KEITH briefly becomes Lord Berners.[56]

K: Salve populi everyone! Have you met Roland, my pet apricot?[57] Oh, what am I like?? Eccentric in the house! [*becomes KEITH again*] This guy! Lord Berners, you are *SUCH* an aesthete! Now, your job, dear audience, is to play the "German audience". Don't panic, it's pretty similar to what you're currently doing, maybe a bit more leather. You're also very sophisticated: you love the avant garde. You've just been sitting listening to music that sounds like this:

BAND smacks the keys of the piano at random.[58]

K: ... for about two hours, and you seemed to enjoy that. You may have just been in the foyer enjoying some German cocktails: perhaps a Gin and Teutonic?

BAND plays a tadah because it was a good joke. Everyone laughs gaily.

K: But seriously, ladies and gentlemen, to be an avant garde German audience, you will need this handy German phrase which I shall teach you. And it goes like this: 'Ich bin höflich aber verwirrt.' Now repeat after me:

> Ich bin höflich aber verwirrt[59]
> Ich bin höflich aber verwirrt
> Ich bin höflich aber verwirrt
> Ich bin höflich aber verwirrt

K: Very good. And it's got a tune as well, and it goes a little bit something like this:

BAND accompanies, and KEITH plays a bit with them ad lib ad hoc to make sure they've got it.

K: And what does that phrase mean? Well of course it means: 'I am polite but confused'. But enough ado, the curtain rises, and the audience prepares to watch the Fifth Marquis of Anglesey presenting the famous 'Electric Butterfly Dance'.[60]

He bids they applaud. They do, with obvious and unalloyed enthusiasm.

Pin-spot on centre stage. HENRY stands, approaching it slowly, full of hope.

'FLAPPING OUT FROM THIS MOMENT'

H: Regrettably,
I am now here.
I will now dance
And disappear.[61]

I will raise one hand
Thus, so.
That's my trembling wing
And this hand, the grass below.

I'm a butterfly.

There is something
I've been trying to say.
Who'd have thought it would
Happen today?

I have always been
Tongue-tied,
Now my soul
Is outside.

I'm a butterfly!

Flapping out from this moment,
Filling all the past with light,
Especially the days
When it was empty and it felt like
Absolutely nothing happened.

But all of that has come to this,
To now, to this, to me.

And when you look at it like that
It all makes sense,
It all has symmetry.

This dance is honest
And clear,
Through wings of coloured glass
I appear.

If you touch the wings
They lose shine,
But for now
They are mine.

I'm a butterfly!

Flapping out from this moment
Filling all the room with light:
Their hearts, their heads
A shower of blazing reds.

And all of me has come to this,
Like a paint blotch on a folded page,
You unfold it, then you see
Its symmetry.

KEITH gets the audience to sing their refrain:

AUD: Ich bin höf-lich aber verwirrt.
Ich bin höf-lich aber verwirrt.
Ich bin höf-lich aber verwirrt.
Ich bin höf-lich aber verwirrt.

H: And I can hear them singing,
Takes away the hurt.
AUD: Ich bin höf-lich aber verwirrt.

H: And I can hear them singing,
Sweet like dessert.
AUD: Ich bin höf-lich aber verwirrt.

H: And I can hear them singing,
A lot of them are called Kurt.
AUD: Ich bin höf-lich aber verwirrt.

H: And they watch and they see and they "get" me,
          See me all the way through
          This is the dance I do:

HENRY enters the spotlight with great dignity. Elegantly and carefully, he does an earnest, meaningless dance: fluttering hands and eyelids, gawky proboscis face; eyes locked hard with the audience, "giving" it so hard to them.

H: Flutterflutterflutterflutter
          Flutterflutterflutterbutter – FLY?

He elegantly turns to face another way.

H: Flutterflutterflutterflutter
          Flutterflutterflutterbutter – FLY?
          CHRYSALIS! CHRYSALIS?

While HENRY is immersed, KEITH (as Berners) goes to leave, very furtively walking in front of as many audients as possible.

K: [*BERNERS*] Come on Roland, if we leave now we can catch last orders [*KEITH*] Oh, Lord Berners, Roland – you're not leaving already? [*BERNERS*] Yes, I've got to... [*KEITH*] Oh. Well what did you think? [*BERNERS*] I thought it was... interesting?... Good luck with it.[62]

Music swells as KEITH (as BERNERS) sweeps out of the door in a puff of faint praise, and KEITH (as KEITH) is left yearning in his wake, arms out-thrust in a Shawshanky manner because this scene is all about him.

K: But Lord Berners, I thought you liked this sort of thing!
          No! No! No! NOOO!

H: Flapping out from this moment,
          Starting butterfly effects and causing
          Storms that turn and burn
          And make tomorrow.

          And finally, I know this is where it all began,
          This moment is a seed, the seed becomes a tree
          Its branches spread, I lift my head and see
          Its symmetry

KEITH generates applause. Or there is silence.

SCENE 6
AN ISSUE OF CASHFLOW

Or "The Cautionary Tale of the Little Boy Who Was Just Too Awesome Yet Had Admittedly Spent the GDP of Chester on Capes".

H: Mr Alexander Keith, did you catch the show?

K: Yes.

H: Did Lord Berners make it?

K: He did.

H: Squee! What did he say?

K: He said it was... it was interesting?

KEITH knows these are platitudes, but HENRY takes it all at face value and is utterly delighted.

H: Oh! What else?

K: And good luck with it.

HENRY is speechless with glee. KEITH breaks the awkwardness by deciding to hear a knock on the door.

K: Hello? Oh? Oh! Oh... Oh. My lord, I just took delivery of a letter, addressed to you and delivered by a man who looked like he was delivering bad news.

H: Give it here.

K: I shall. [*He gives HENRY the mime letter*] What does it say?

H: I cannot, I cannot read it. What does it say?

HENRY fails to give KEITH the mime letter back, but KEITH carries on anyway. HENRY is subtly impressed that KEITH can read this letter from all the way over there.

K: It says 'Dear Marquis, I am writing to you to tell you the very important news that you are ruined. Thanks to your fantastical levels of spending [*HENRY looks pleased*] and I mean "thanks" in a sarcastic way [*HENRY looks serious*] you have no money or cash, just a huge amount of pointless stuff. And now at the age of twenty-nine you must auction it all away to pay off this literally stupid amount of debt. Signed your accountant, whose name is obviously already known to you so I shall not bother to write it here. No kisses.'

They both find the lack of kisses devastating.

HENRY is very serious; experiencing unfamiliar and potentially exciting dramatic experiences.

H: I see. Yes! As it should be. Well, auction it off, auction it all off[63], I need none of it. I will simply sit here and think a while on my golden thinking throne.

K: No, we have to auction that off.

H: Fine, I'll just get out of your way and go to the East Wing and hang out with my favourite peacocks.

K: No, both the East Wing and the peacocks have also to be sold.

H: [*the cogs whirr very slowly*] Maa-kes sense... Well, in that case better just slip on my silver proactivity plimsolls, get on my horse and –

K: No, the horse is –

H: Way ahead of you, no horse, just the –

K: No plimsolls –

H: *Difficult!* [*pause*] But good, well if I must move out, I shall just buy a new house –

K: [*sings*] Henry, there is no money.

B: Sorry what?

BAND starts to get up to leave, KEITH implores in whispers that he stay. BAND indicates that in that case he wants HENRY's helmet, which KEITH hands over. BAND puts it on and sits back down, resplendent but still completely impassive.

H: [*flickers of rage*] Fine. What I will do then, Mr Keith, is I will give up!

K: No!

H: Totally yes, I will give up.

K: But what about... what about *history*?

H: History is crap! I hate it. You can't win.

K: But what about the prophecy? Huge things! Won't it anger those two ghosts from the future or space?

H: Y'see I don't think they were real ghosts. Actually.

K: Auh! But you can't give up.

H: Watch me! I will give up so flipping hard. I will retire, in exile, to live like a peasant – a pauper – in Monte Carlo.

Powerful musical sting. Ominousness.

H: So, Mr Keith... the time has come to stick to that first rule of theatre.

K: Ah! The show must go on.

H: No, the other one.

K: It's not over til the fat lady sings.

H: The other one.

K: Pretend to be your character.

H: The *first* rule.

K: Say all your lines in order.

H: No.

K: The *first* rule?

H: Yes.

K: Turn up... to the theatre?

H: Well, no not –

K: Get people cards on opening night?

H: Sorry.

K: Don't say your mum's name instead of Juliet.

H: What?

K: Whoever's on the poster's the best.

H: No.

K: If you shave your head you're really serious.

H: Damn it.

K: The interval's not long enough to go to the toilet!

H: No. I speak of the other other other other other other other other other other first rule of theatre: Give the people what they want.

K: Ar, of course! But, what do people want?

H: Come to me Alexander Keith.

KEITH kneels before HENRY elegantly in the style of Shakespeare's Globe. HENRY kneels too, then does a beautiful gesture right up in KEITH's face.

H: It's truth. Will you do me this? Tell the people of this heavy velvet land the truth about me. While I? I will board this ship...

HENRY points to a massive ship just behind him. KEITH realises that holy cats there's a massive ship just behind HENRY.

H: ... to the aforementioned Monte Carlo where I will live out a pitiful gap-year-style existence of humbleness and incredible poverty cheekbones. And so, goodbye. Or, as the French say: 'au revoir'.

K: Oh, but doesn't that mean 'until we meet again'?

H: Oh yeah you're right, so not that then.

HENRY begins to reverse up an invisible gangplank, waving.

K: No, Henery, don't! And he has gone.

HENRY goes into neutral i.e. turns around and pretends that you can't see him.

This page intentionally left blank

SCENE 7
ALONE AGAIN, AND

In which our other, non-main hero takes the narrative reins into his own hand, and in the other hand takes a metaphorical Vuvuzela of encouragement.

K: And I am alone again. But what was it he said?

H: [*in KEITH's imagination*] Incredible poverty cheekbones!

K: Before that.

H: [*ditto*] Tell them the truth!

K: Correct. But how do I do that? Think, you magnificent pile of Keith.

KEITH sets off on a journey. HENRY also sets off on a journey. They are both on journeys.

'KEITH'S QUEST'[64]

K: I'll travel round the world,
         By which I mean Britain.
HB: Britain!
K: Performing a one-man show
         Which I will have written.
HB: Will have written!
H: Laugh at Henry, point at Henry,
         Take his stuff, evict him.
         Now I know what I was born to be
         i.e. a victim.
K: It is now ten minutes from the end, it
         Is high time for me to be to be sended
         On a mission to make things splendid.
H: But will it get better for a happy ending?
K: My name is Mr Alexander Keith, and this is... Keith's Quest.

The whole vista of the Britannic Kingdom of Isles opens up before KEITH, and he advances on it like when Robin Hood runs from Dover to Nottingham via Hadrian's Wall in like a day in the Kevin Costner one. Meanwhile, HENRY's ship casts off and sails into a sad sunset, except South because he's going to France. I mean practically speaking what actually happens is they jab their hands this way and that in time to the music while the rest of it is done with lighting.

HKB: Keith's Quest, Keith's Quest,
K: Now it's time to go on
HKB: Keith's Quest, Keith's Quest,
K: My heart pounding under

HKB: 'Neath vest, 'derneath vest,
K: I need to stop and have a
HKB: Rest...

He has a breather, and a quick sip of drink. But then he's back!

K: Then carry on
HKB: Keith's Quest.

K: I will travel to all the places: Wales, England,
Peterborough, Scotland,
The other one, and Cornwall, and the North.
HB: Keith's Quest!
K: Hey you there!

The BAND gives his 'Geordie Lass'.

B: Oh! Y'areet pet?
K: What comes into your mind when I say the name
Henry Cyril Paget?[65]
B: Oh, nothing pet.
K: Right. Let me tell you about him then.
HKB: Keith's Quest!
B: Oh! So will you buy us a drink then like pet?
K: Oh. Yeah, sure why not... I guess.

HKB: Keith's Quest, Keith's Quest
B: Will you buy us a drink?
HK: I guess, I guess
HKB: This show'll be areet pet, areet pet,
K: There's some tickets left in Neath, best
HKB: Check with the box office.

HENRY glides forward as though on a revolve. Or, if we have a revolve, on a revolve.

H: He-nry's jour-ney,
He-nry's jour-ney,
Be-ing hu-mble:
Learny learny lea-rny.

We split-screen between the two of them, using lights and showbiz.

K: // Keith's Quest, Keith's Quest,
It's an actor's greatest test, greatest test.

Everybody is impressed, everybody is impressed
By the way I move and talk, and
The way I do Keith's Quest.

H: // He-nry's jour-ney,
He-nry's jour-ney,
Be-ing hu-mble:
Learny learny lea-rny.

HKB: Keith's Quest, Keith's Quest, Keith's Quest

K: And now in Welsh!

KEITH is orating from the top of Snowdon or like gets up on some steps if he can.

HENRY dubs KEITH, as in KEITH mimes to HENRY, not as in HENRY makes KEITH Sir KEITH.

K (H): Heidiwch, dewch, mynychwch, Gymry'n gwlwm,[66]
Ymddangosaf yn eich plith fel rhith.
Dwi'n mynd i ddeud y gair "astronaut" rŵan am ddim rheswm.
Na pharabler; ustiwch. Canys fi...

K: ... di Keith

KEITH mimes different modes of transport which all look basically the same.

HB: Ke-ith Ke-e-ith
K: I am riding on a horse!
HB: Ke-ith Ke-e-ith
K: I am driving a train!
HB: Ke-ith Ke-e-ith
K: I am a passenger in a hot air balloon or something, I don't know
HB: Ke-ith Ke-e-ith!
K: I am checking into a hotel
I'm tired!

HKB: This is Keith's Quest, Keith's Quest.
This chorus is the briefest:
Keith's Quest.

Split screen again.

KB: I want to be a piston,
              Riding from Cockermouth / to Penistone

H: / What do people want?

KB: Shooting from the Gorbals, bang into Hornsea
              I will even visit Swansea.

H: This is what it / looks like

KB: / Bringing you the straight-up,
              Masculine truth.

HENRY does the 'taptaptap' of a location appearing at the bottom of the screen in the X-Files.

B: A village hall *somewhere* in Britain.

K: Good evening Didcot.

BAND becomes a medium-sized room full of people from the past with values systems also from the past.

B: Hello.

K: Hello crowd. Friends, womans, countrymen, lend me some ears.

B: Sound of that happening.

K: Thank you. It is I, Mr Keith, and I come to you tonight suspended on a hopeful limb
to tell you about he whom I have followed for between two and four years.
But I come not to praise Henry Cyril Paget...

B: Expectant intake.

K: But to super-ultra praise him.

B: Spontaneous approval.

K: So this is it, the truth, the whole Keith truth and nothing but the Keith.

B: Significant gasp! Woman faints.

K: Henry Cyril Paget, well –

B: Yes?

K: – he *is* a little bit... funny, if you know what I mean.

Pause.

B: Urgh.

K: Oh no! Ha, I mean. Well, you know... if you know what I mean.

B: In this time period we don't really have the vocabulary.

K: Yes, but you DO know what I mean.

B: Widespread fainting.

K: No it's not like that, he's different...

B: He makes us feel very heteronormative.

K: What?

B: It means good.

K: He makes you feel good?

B: No, not being him makes us feel good.

K: Oh, but...

B: I blame a lax upbringing. And that European waltz music.

K: No, no, no! Let me just get my visual aid. There! You see.

KEITH shows a photograph of HENRY in a really very silly pose.

K: This is what he looks like...
B: That is what he looks like?
K: Isn't it...
B: Appalling.
K: Appealing?
B: Appalling.
K: Fuck.
B: / *Look* at him, *look* at him, *look* at him, *look* at him...
K: / No, please. Please. Just –

KB: Look at him...
B: The silly fool decked
           Out like some cray-cray bee.

H: Look at me!

KB: Look at him...

B: I literally cannot
Process what my eyes see.

H: Look at me!

KB: Look at him...

B: That's a man no British
Boy would ever, ever want
To be.

K: Look at him.

B: Look at that.

H: Like this?

KB: Look at him!

H: I am a narcissist!

K: Look at me destroying this man who
Gave me lots of money.

H: Narcissist!

KB: Look at him!

B: His stupid, dancing
Face he is so funny, he goes:

HB: Oh la de da de da

KB: This is him!

HB: Oh la de da de
Da

H: M-wah.

HENRY vanishes.

B: Thank you for bringing us news of this monstrous woof.

K: No!
What have I *done*?
[*trying out different line readings*] What *have* I done?
What... have I done?

This is what it looks like
To be a Judas type character
Such as Agamemnon, Edward Snowden,
Or Edmund from Narnia!

HKB: Quest failed!

KEITH drags himself away with a purgatorial lighting cue.

This page intentionally left blank

SCENE 8
A GLIMMER OF HOPE IN A SEA OF YACHTS

In which a simple wind ensemble is a catalyst for change.

Enter Monte Carlo. Enter HENRY, in basic Monte Carlo fashions. We are in Monte Carlo.

H: And so, finally, here I am in cold, forbidding Monte Carlo with some sort of lung thing [*koff*]. Alone, and with nothing but between one and no years left to live.

BAND and KEITH play the Eton School Song from earlier on mime brass instruments. It is a bit Brassed Off.

H: But wait, what is that sound I hear from out on that balcony?

HENRY opens the door to the balcony, the brass swells in volume.

H: Yes, look down there on the Avenue de Monte Carlo – which is the main street here in Monte Carlo – that small wind ensemble and their tuba-playing friend are playing my old school song. That never fails to rouse me.

HENRY grimaces, shuts the door, brass diminishes.

H: Gah, but no. Even that cheerfully military tune now actually makes me feel a bit... sad. It's music for a man whom I will never bem. Men of certainty, courage, affableness, doing REAL things in red chinos and a polo shirt. All I can do is froof! and ponce! and... pretend.

KB: [*very loud sotto*] Pretend!

H: [*sotto*] Pretend?

HENRY suddenly has fire and sass spark in his eyes. He has just realised something.

H: I've just realised something.

B: [*sotto*] What?

H: I'm going to win.[67]

BAND and KEITH continue to mime-brass the Eton School Song (they have got to "I want to join...") and HENRY sings a descant / cerdd dant[68] over the top.

'IN THE MORNING (SCHOOL SONG (REPRISE))'

H: I totally now know what I must a-do,[69]
Not right now, but in the morning and without further ado,
Before I die of some sort of lung thing,
In the morning I'll get one shot to fix everything.
Soon it will be all flowers and j'adore-ments,
For I am about to give my greatest and arguably finalest
performa-ance

I will be
[*slight*] Normal, [*incredibly ornate vocal gymnastics*] no-
o-ormal-uh.
No sleep tonight, I'm Nessun Dormal, but
Clever Classic FM jokes aside,
I'm about to commit preconceptionicide.
Look into the future – bang! – I'm in it,
You. Mind. Blown in a minute

*KEITH flies a tweed jacket in and effortlessly en-dons HENRY with it
while also being the sound of cocks on the horizon.*

H: In the morning,
KB: Cock a doodle do!
H: In the morning!
KB: Cock a doodle do!
H: Can I have some toast please?
K: Baguette, sir?
H: No I can't, I'm too nervous.
K: Of course.

This page intentionally left blank

SCENE 9
TWEED

In which it's not a Daily Fail, it's a Daily Succeed.

H: And so, at the age of twenty-nine, what I thought I'd do was do an interview with the *Daily Mail*. I know! I thought if I could just "be myself" and show them the "real me", then we could make a "connection". You see, you should always try very hard to "connect" with another human being. Or a *Daily Mail* journalist.

Enter KEITH as a slavering tongue-based bat columnist called Quentin. They be seated.

K: Well your grace, I suppose let's start with what we're all wondering, how are you?

An extravagant swirl of an intro on the piano, but HENRY ignores it. Instead, he speaks "normally" for the first time. He is nervous, delicate, but is playing his part well.

H: Good morning Quentin. First off, I must apologise for not appearing before you in a peacock-blue plush wearing a diamond and sapphire tiara, a turquoise dog-collar, ropes of pearls and slippers studded with Burma rubies; but I prefer – and have always preferred – Scotch tweed.[70]

K: Tweed? You mean to tell me that you like wearing that most civilised, normal, masculine of textiles: *TWEED*?

H: Yes. I love tweed...

KEITH looks down to scribble notes; HENRY takes an opportunity...

H: [*to an audience member*] I do not like tweed.

KEITH looks up; HENRY snaps back to him. Caught?

H: It's... just a thing I like. Like? I mean love. What is it? Tweed!

KEITH looks down at his notes.

H: [*to audience*] I do not like it even a tiny bit, AHAHAHAA!

KEITH snaps up again and so does HENRY; he is getting good at this.

H: It's just, you know. Wow: tweed.

KEITH takes a little longer to look down, but hesitates, and nearly fakes HENRY out twice. He eventually goes.

H: [*to audience*] Not wow, not tweed, I HATE it: it makes me come out in a rash and the rash spells out 'ew gross tweed' on my face, in rash.

KEITH snaps up again, but HENRY's all over this and turns perfectly to meet him, smiling.

H: It's just a sensible choice.

K: What is it exactly about tweed that you love so much?

H: Me?

K: Yes.

H: [*gags a bit on the word*] ... texture.

K: Texture?

H: [*the word tastes bad*] cccolour?

K: Hmm.

H: Oh and that seam. You know? That sticks in, just *there*, so when you're walking and you're sweating and you're walking and sweating and the seam's just "good evening!" and it reminds you always always that hey you're angry but you don't know WHY!

HENRY's passion rather overtakes him, and he leaps to his feet.

H: I mean in an ideal world (I mean one can dream, can't one Quentin?) I'd have literally everything of tweed: trouser of tweed, jacket of tweed, pant of tweed, pancreas, man face, lungs... I mean a tweed suit of armour's what I really need, so I can go marching up and down the world, blowing away all those non-tweed natives in their tweedless national dress. TWEEDOOM! CHAKKATWEEDOOM! And they all run around saying 'I'm so sorry Henry, we should have worn the TWEED! EHE EEE-E-E-E- -EEE-EEE-EE-... d!'

Pause of regalvanisation. Then HENRY launches into a Minnie the Moocher esque zoot suit strut.

H: A TWEEDY WEEDY TWEEDY TWEEDY TWEEDY TOODAH, ahhhhh...

HENRY suddenly realises what he's doing, regrets and freezes in shameful freeze. KEITH glares at him for a hot painful moment.

K: Thank you. That is more than enough. The article will appear in the morning. [*licks quill*] I am *astonished* to find a man so extraordinarily... eurghhhhhmmmmm... the same as other men are, whose tastes and lack of intellect have been enormously exaggerated.

'NORMAL, NORMAL (SCHOOL SONG (REPRISE (REPRISE)))'

K: He is
Normal, normal,
The kind of bloke who'd take you to a rugby club formal
(If you were a young lady, obviously).
By the old school tie here knotted,
By George, I think he's got it.
Hashtag have a nice day,
Quentin away!

KEITH flies away on stony, leathery wings, off to presumably enact ancient prophecy in another location linked only by geography and Quentin.

HENRY is flabbergasted, and does a triumphant pose.

SCENE 10
REGRETTABLE

In which a reunion happens, then an ending, and then history.

Slowly building arpeggios, as HENRY walks with a new peace through Monte Carlo.

H: And so I went back to my humble Monte Carlo abode with a spring in my step.

HENRY does a low-key Artful Dodger-style skip. It is a move that is enjoyed by, on average, 1.5 audience members.

HENRY opens a mime door into his apartment, and exhales. Someone wearing a bustle sweeps in.

K: Hello again Henry.

H: Oh hi Lilian. "You're looking well", "thanks for coming".[71]

K: "Thanks". So you're wearing tweed now?

H: Yes. "It's a long story".

K: So.

H: So.

K: I hear you're "dying".

H: Oh, yes. Yes I'm "dying".

K: "Shall we then?"

H: "Shall we?"

K: "Come here Henry"

H: And so I walked over to her,
And I put my head in her hands.

K: And he coughed, and he held up his hand
To guard against the window's light.

KEITH cradles a mime HENRY, but he has not gone to her.

H: This is what it looks like
To look up and to sigh,

HK: This is what it looks like,
This is what it looks like
To die.

KEITH[72] and BAND leave.

HENRY is alone, with a glassy half-smile.

He rips off the tweed and flings it on the floor.

Hesitantly, he goes to the piano.

He picks up playing where BAND left off, with a basic level of competence that somehow surprises us. Everything is sweet.

'I SORT OF WON'

H: And so I died.[73]
Yes, I died.
And it was AMAZING,
So realistic,
You should've been there.
Amazing, amazing
Death.

So I sort of won.
I mean, regrettably they burnt every trace of me,
Every photograph, every letter, every document
In a fire.
They burnt me out of their history
And that was REGRETTABLE.

A ferocity starts to overcome HENRY, and soon he is roaring in the gathering darkness.

H: But I *was* rich
And I *was* an aristocrat
And I *was* worried,
But I was certain.
I was lonely
But I was fierce:
I was a cro-oss,
I was a cro-oss,
I was a cross dresser,
I was a cross dresser,
I was one, I was one, I was that!
And so...

I sort of won.

YES!
I sort of won, if you really think about it.
God, if you really, *really* think about it.

I sort of, sort of, sort of,
Sort of!
I SORT OF WON![74]

HENRY snatches at the air. Lights flare up briefly behind him. A hard blackout.

END.

FEETNOTE

1   Mr Keith is in the group photo near the beginning of this book, proving that (a) he existed, and (b) showed up on film, therefore probably wasn't a vampire. In addition, he was also indeed the actor-manager of the Gaiety, Henry's chapel-cum-theatre. That's pretty much all I know.

However, a friend a while back gave me the gift of a lovely teatowel, reproducing the poster for the Gaiety's production of Aladdin which was "specially written" by Mr Keith, to be performed "On Monday, June 2nd, 1902, and every evening until further notice". The whole thing is jam packed with period, end-of-the-pier racistyness, wordplay and dad jokes, and that sort of thing gave us a start on the character. I'll put the teatowel in this book so you can see it (I mean a picture of it, obviously).

2   In the words of Clough Williams-Ellis, the architect who designed Portmeirion (which is a pretendy town of follies and facades of picturesque Italian campitude in Gwynedd, N Wales, and which is most famous for being the location of 60s prisoner-based surreal thriller, *The Prisoner*, but which is famous to me for having been visited by me several times as a kid, spending most of the time scanning balconies for good places to have an athletic swordfight) Henry was: "a sort of apparition – a tall, elegant and bejeweled creature, with wavering elegant gestures, reminding one rather of an Aubrey Beardsley illustration come to life." Which I should probably have just put as the stage direction.

3   This is correct and definitely was his name. He was also Earl of Uxbridge, Lord Anglesey, called himself Lord Paget and apparently had the intriguing nickname "Toppy". Which is intriguing.

4   Estates in Staffs, Dorset, Anglesey and Derbyshire and an income of £11 million per year in 2017 money.

5   As I said in the Foreword, Marquis # I was a Waterloo hero guy and also apparently a bit of a lad, reputedly saying as he had his leg cut off (without anaesthetic): "I have had a pretty long run. I have been a beau these 47 years and it would not be fair to cut the young men out any longer." The other former Marquisi seem to have variously spent their time being called Henry (they are all called Henry), founding cricket clubs, being Staffordshire MPs, grenadier guards and to have generally Marquised in a fairly conventional manner. However, it seems that there's a theme with two of them of running off with women while with wife. Marquis I (*The Phantom Menace*), whom *The Complete Peerage* described as "a brilliant, gallant cavalry officer, but neither a wise nor a virtuous man", eloped with, and eventually married, another woman while already having 100% of the number of allowed wives. The brother of Charlotte Cadogan, the intended second wife, challenged him to a duel for the besmirchment of their family honour, and so the two men shot guns at each other without any real consequence in Wimbledon one day. Paget's 'second' (i.e. sort of his backup I guess) in the duel was a man called Hussey Vivian, the 1st Baron Vivian – who, I've got to be honest here, has a name I could say all day. Then Marquis IV (*The Kingdom of the Crystal Skull*) decided that as a third sequel he needed to up his game considerably, but with sad and horrible consequences. To be continued in Footnote 22.

6   Dates: 16 June 1875 – 14 March 1905.

7   "Penniless" is of course relative, but yes. More on this just before he dies.

8   This is also true, more on the Gaiety Theatre slightly sooner than that.

9   Also true, although of course anything that was already in the public domain will have escaped the pyre.

10 This isn't actually an obituary but his official entry in *The Complete Peerage*, which is pretty brutal. I thought it'd be clearer in the midst of the information barrage at the top of the show to bend that a bit. Also, I thought the actual obituaries would bum people out too much. I mean check this one out from the *Daily Dispatch*: "From his earliest recollection he had been one of those extraordinarily isolated creatures who have never known affection. From boyhood to death no one had ever loved him... [from which he developed] a strange and repellent spirit opaquely incomprehensible and pathetically alone... Over it all was the self-conscious, half-haughty timidity of the man who knows he is not as other men.". Jeez Louise, Dispatch, have a snack or something, you're grumpy. This one from *The Times* is nicer though: "The news of Lord Anglesey's death was received at Bangor with much regret, as Lord Anglesey, despite his peculiarities, was much liked there."

11 Queen Victoria (Queen of Britain slash England, Thingy of India, Empress of Space etc) unhelpfully died on 22nd Jan 1901, meaning that this story bridges the Victorian and Edwardian era making references quite confusing. It wasn't the most inconsiderate thing she did, sure, but it's up there.

12 In an earlier draft of the show Matthew, playing Keith, had to do a lot more different accents, including a whirling kaleidoscope of dialects leading into what is now Scene 1, where we hypno-regressed the audience through the early scenes of Henry's life. In a very real sense, Matthew in this draft is getting off *very* lightly.

13 She could have. For my money the door is still very open. "Geordie Lass" from Scene 7, e.g., is a meaty role.

14 Okay so. With the aforementioned early life sequence – featuring a carnival of accents – cut, there's some stuff to fill in here. This account, from Henry's childhood friend (so he had one. Relief.), as quoted by Prof Viv Gardner in a *Guardian* article, covers much of it: "He was then about eight years of age and of delicate appearance. Having at the age of two lost his mother, Toppy, as he was called by his intimate friends, never enjoyed that influence so prized by and so valuable to all, that of one's unselfish loving mother. An aged Scotch nurse of pious life was the first person I remember to have been his companion, and often they would be seen walking or driving in a pony carriage. Little time was spent with British boys of his own age. Unfortunate surroundings in youth tended to make him perhaps a little un-English." This is a reference to a rumour that followed him around: that he was the illegitimate son of famed French actor Benoit Coquelin, owing to the fact that when Henry's mother, Blanche Mary Curwen Boyd, died, Henry did some living in France with Coquelin's sister-in-law.

For what it's worth, this seems to be a concoction based on a misunderstanding, as the sister-in-law in question was also Henry's maternal aunt (because people can be two things). But who cares about that, there was a general sense that even if no bastarding had in fact happened, then being exposed to French people had definitely made him into the show-off he obviously was. I mean imagine all the accents there would have been in this bit! French! Scottish! Dying mother! Some cuts are a tragedy, honestly.

15 There is no evidence he had a bunk mate called Cameron, though he did go to Eton, which will surprise nobody.

16 Henry actually became a Lieutenant in the 2nd Volunteer Battalion of the Royal Welsh Fusiliers. I have no idea how that panned out though; I'm imagining it was a bit like when I went to a Cub Scout Jamboree.

17 If you don't know what Eton is, then just imagine Hogwarts with magic swapped for money, and with an equally tiresome preoccupation with vigorous outdoor sport.

18 I went to Ysgol Gyfun Llangefni comprehensive, so my only knowledge of fagging is entirely theoretical. It is, I gather, like a buddying system except with the opposite of buddying. An unbuddying system where, as a younger boy, you become an older boy's slave. We didn't have it. We just had reputed occasional bog-washes (head in toilet while flush) and the ever-vibrant rumour of a disused swimming pool under the school hall.

19 This was a Conservative Party slogan from 2009: an age when – as now – we really very much weren't. This is a very subtle and sophisticated bit of satire I put in for eagle-eared viewers, made even more piquant by the fact that the Conservative Party leader was in fact once called Cameron! I'm awaiting your call, The Now Show.

20 Yep, I'm insecure enough to make my characters give positive reviews of songs I've written. Five stars.

21 This was Blanche Mary Boyd, who died in 1877, when he was two, resulting in him living in Paris til he was eight.

22 According at least to a salacious article in *The Baltimore Sun* in 1902, Marquis IV met the American Mrs Wetmore while still married to his second wife, Blanche Mary (Henry's mother). I couldn't find Mrs Wetmore's first name initially as all sources had her as 'Mrs William Wetmore' because patriarchy, but Prof Viv Gardner, mighty thing-knower from the University of Manchester that she is, instructs me her first name was Annie. I'm not sure how she knows, probably because she has *spies in the past*. Anyway, Marquis IV promised to marry her once Blanche had died, even telling Mrs W to get a wedding dress, and Mrs W duly left her current husband for him. But by then Paget had got bored of her, and married another American woman he'd met, Mary "Minna" King. Annie tried to sue him, but "The Marquis did not even take the trouble to repudiate the allegation with regard to the promise, but contented himself with pointing out that as the offense had been committed in France he could not be tried in England, and that there is no law punishing breach of promise in France."

And so Mrs Wetmore killed herself with poison. That a year or so later Paget left Minna anyway will come as little surprise. By this point even The British Royal Family (champions of the underdog that they are) decided to step in by very pointedly and valiantly sending the Duke & Duchess of Connaught to dine with the newly-divorced Marchioness several times in Paris *instead of with the Marquis*, which is Not Something They Do, which is why the patriarchy doesn't exist any more hooray *waves tiny flag*.

As a further twist, there is a sad allegation, which I found in *The Des Moines Register*, that Blanche Mary's death had also been at her own hand. If this is all true – and that is of course a chunk of 'if' – then it paints quite a cruel, cold, capricious picture, that the man Henry (our Henry: they really are all called Henry) would've been raised to idolise was one who was far from overflowing with the milk of human not-being-a-dick-to-women-ness. An intriguing vignette however, from the *Baltimore Sun* article again, suggests the faintest glimmer that Marquis IV had at least some self-knowledge: "Upon one occasion he ordered a large collection of new patent fire extinguishers for his country place. After the butler had arranged them all over the house he told the Marquis that there were a dozen left over. 'Put them in my coffin,' said the Marquis; 'I shall need them.'"

23   I think it's statistically unlikely that an aristocratic mother in 1877 would have said this.

24   I sadly cannot confirm that Henry was visited by ghosts. Only heavily assume.

25   The ghosts' section has gone through the most edits. They've been given and lost two long numbers. The first, *The Lips of Destiny*, was the first thing we made when Matthew and I first started making this show (way back when we were even more young and emerging than we still definitely are): an inspirational disco number we loved until an audience member (Matthew's partner) pointed out that it's actually just the theme tune to *Blake's Seven*. Which it was. They then got given a song called *Nobody Really Knows What They're Doing*, a gospelly one in which the ghosts gleefully admitted they had no idea how to ghost, and was about the general suspicion one can get that everyone in the world is really just bodging it; copying what other people like them seem to do. I miss that one – it filled in a bit in Henry's journey of learning to live by pretending. It might return.

26   And he did. As the *Saint Paul Globe* of Minnesota pithily noted in its obituary: "He perfumed his automobile with violets. He wore primroses in his hair. He wore women's clothing." – way to bury the lead, *Globe*. I mean it's sort of an obituary, while also at the same time being an article about how "Former St Paul Man" Almeric Hugh Paget could be in line to become Marquis VI (*The Undiscovered Country*) with Henry dead, but in fact spends *a long* time talking about silken menswear in terms spiralling from grumpy ("There was no splendor, however barbaric, that the eccentric young marquis did not attempt to achieve, no extravagance he was unwilling to attempt") to downright breathless ("The pajamas and night shirts were dreams of oriental splendor").

One of the most dressy of the actual 'dress' dresses we've got pictures of is the one he wears as Queen Eleanor – one of his top fave queens apparently – which will have come up on your Google earlier. It's the one where he's sat on a chair on a carpet in a dress in the garden about to casually pluck off his own head like that's completely standard. It wasn't all dresses though; he could turn his hand to a number of looks, and seems to have pleasingly blurred the boundary between 'outfit' and 'costume'. As reported in the delightfully-named *Omaha Daily Bee* (a daily bee? a bee *every* day! Gadzooks, what brave new world, Omaha, that has such bees in it?): "He is a thoroughly effeminate looking young fellow and he may be seen when in Paris walking around with a toy terrier under his arm, the pet having been heavily scented and bedizened with bangles and bows. The fingers of the marquis fairly blaze with rings. He presents the characteristics of the Gypsy type." 'Bedizened' is now your word of the day forever – you're welcome.

27 So this pause lasts about fifteen years (in theatrical time, I mean. In real time, it's much less) during which Henry learns painting and singing in Germany, and learns fluent French, good Russian and grammatical Welsh.

In the movie version, there would be a training montage featuring a dance / modern languages teacher played by an Imelda Staunton / Sandi Toksvig type in a blazer who would be initially aghast at his dancing, then delighted, and then finally aghast again. Then, when he turned twenty-one, his family threw The Biggest My Sweet Sixteen Except You're Twenty One Party Of All Ever. This, apparently in addition to a shindig and a half probably involving a buffet which, laid end-to-end, could reach to Aberystwyth and back five times, also involved villages all round the island bunting up their streets for the birthday boy to parade through, being adored. Well, wouldn't you adore an aristocrat who marched through your town every time they had a Big Birthday? Wouldn't you be out there, your favourite confetti burning a hole in your giddy little fist? No, me neither.

Potensh then it's a slight mercy that Henry missed the whole thing because he was bedridden with illness; I take it the same illness that would kill him eightish years later. But (and this is the crucial bit) the family went ahead with the party without him. Which I have mixed feelings about: imagining him feverish in bed, the thudding bass of a jungle remix of "The Lost Chord" by Arthur Sullivan floating over from the marquee, is heartsqueezy. However, it does appeal in a weird way to my inbuilt Methodistish frugality. I mean they'd already paid for it anyway, so...

28 No worries, I did it already. 16th Century painter; done many pictures of women with reddish-gold hair. I imagine this wouldn't have been his number one aim as an artist, but his name became synonymous, in certain circles, with this colour of hair, to the extent that in the 60s, Barbies with red hair were officially labelled "Titian". Lilian was said to have such big eyes and such a generally golden colouring, that she was given the nickname 'The Goldfish', which was a compliment, apparently.

29 And yet we shall. Lady Florence Paget was so small and beautiful that she was given the nickname 'The Pocket Venus'. I mean we're probably more talking a newspaper nickname here rather than something you'd use in

normal conversation, like "Oh hi 'The Pocket Venus', here's that watering can you were looking for. Careful, don't fall in!". But anyway, her mythic aura of love and sense of portability made her a must for any party, opera or croquet match. But, when she had been due to marry Henry Chaplin, a buddy of the Prince of Wales, she instead had a scandalous dalliance with the Marquis of Hastings in Marshall and Snelgrove's department store, and then eloped with him.

He turned out to have the nickname 'The Wicked Marquis', which she maybe didn't know about, but which he vigorously lived up to, and gambled and drank himself to death, leaving her a widow at twenty-six. A widow who, because of what she'd done to that poor Prince of Wales's friend guy, all of polite society now shunned and wouldn't let her anywhere near their pockets.

When it came to her second husband, it became clear that perhaps she was just into compulsive gamblers, because he was a compulsive gambler. Their marriage was not fun, apparently, but she did have four kids, one of whom was Lilian. Florence took one look at her Titian hair and decided that Titian hair was a sure sign of weak character. Thus it was that she set up the match with the man who couldn't possibly lead her daughter into disrepute: Henry Cyril Paget.

30 It was, and they were. Lady Florence had the surname Paget. Dead giveaway.

31 The thing the two of them do with the air quotes is supposed to be a playful sort of shared eye-roll 'aren't grown ups lame they're like nuh nuh nuh' contact that two kids might share when they're going through the motions of a ritual of polite society. At the same time it carries on the theme of Henry learning to ape surface behaviour, of pretending, as a means of fitting in. It was important to me that in our version of the story, there's the chance that this relationship might actually somehow work – albeit as friends – and that they could learn to play the system to their advantage. And possibly make each other happy. Also, having them join in together instinctively with this game means that Henry gets at least a little bit of chemistry with another human being.

32 There's a definition of the word 'camp' which I heard once and liked and then have never been able to attribute. By which I mean every time I say it people are like I've not heard that and it doesn't come up on Google. The definition is "to walk as though walking, to drink a cup of tea as though drinking a cup of tea". Which I take to mean that you do a thing, while also at the same time *performing* it. Like you're sort of doing a Michael Mcintyre observational comedy thing about the chicken kiev you're eating, while you're eating a chicken kiev. Or a bit like when you're drunk and suddenly the way your friend looks at her watch is really funny, and then it's suddenly impossible for her to look at her watch in any way that isn't hilarious. Or like when someone tells you to 'act natural' and that immediately becomes impossible. In more fancydoodle terms, it's a way of revealing the fundamental absurdity of pretty much the whole of everything.

It's a very fun filter to live your life through, I find. Several times, I've been in a sub-ideal situation, like freezing outside a dark, rural train station at 3am in February; or in a hotel in Hull with a television literally nailed to the chipboard wall and the furniture's all laminated, and the manager is cantering around the hallways announcing that he is drunk although we are all clear on that, and there are three drawers in the empty breakfast room and they are labelled "KNIVES", "FORKS, SPOONS" and "GRAVY SAUCE"; and I've entertained myself by thinking 'Wouldn't it be funny if this was actually happening in real life?' It's either a bit zen, or the absolute opposite of a bit zen, and I don't feel qualified to say which. In any case, the original draft of this song was called *To Kiss As Though We're Kissing (As Though There's Nothing Missing)*, which is why I brought it up in the first place.

33 #maths #edutainment #yourewelcome

34 This is of course a reference to *The Golden Girls*, a key mid-to-late 80s sitcom brought to you by the power of shoulder pads, embroidered tracksuits and women of a certain age. Ten points for getting that. Actually, it's pretty entry-level: five.

35 One thing that Henry was actually known for was copying and mimicry. He would dress up as sort of glam versions of various national archetypes / stereotypes, as well as specific figures. A Berlin paper commented that "the likeness of the German Emperor and the German heroes of the last decades were beautifully rendered". He also appeared in Munich performing something billed as "lightning change impersonations and side-splitting imitations", according to *The Des Moines Register*. This act – an aristocrat doing funny impressions of aristocrats – seems (funnily enough) to have gone down well with other aristocrats, as the *Register* continues: "Anglesey startled a number of his friends one night in impersonating a dashing society woman of the Lady Gay Spanker order, and the next day he had half a dozen good offers to take it up professionally." 'Lady Gay Spanker' is surprisingly not-not-safe-for-work as Googles go. She's a character in the Dion Boucicault 1841 comedy *London Assurance*, and is a bit like a cross between Lord Flashheart from *Blackadder* and Princess Anne, or at least she was when Fiona Shaw was playing her.

36 The word 'realness', as well as a fair bit of the wordage in this bit, comes, to me at least – and if you're reading this there's a moderate chance you already know this – from the television delight *RuPaul's Drag Race*, in which (predominantly) American drag queens of various aesthetic and performative factions compete to be the best drag queen by embodying the virtues of Charisma, Uniqueness, Nerve and Talent. And, obviously, also have substantial and elaborate fights with much waving of arm and casting asunder of wig. That programme in turn borrowed from the veryimportantseminal but also incredibly good documentary *Paris is Burning*, by Jennie Livingstone, about the drag scene of late 80s New York.

It's quite hard to adequately describe, but basically you've got a clutch of astoundingly creative queer people, pushed to the underground – many having been thrown out of their homes and taken in by elder queens who protect and nurture them – holding lavish drag contests, or 'balls', in the wee hours of the morning in public meeting halls; strutting on makeshift catwalks in phenomenal outfits fashioned out of what little stuff they could pull together. 'Drag' in this context is a broad church, of which dressing up as an exaggerated female character – what we'd conventionally refer to as drag queens – are only one category. 'Drag' is an overarching term for visually emulating any group: there's military drag, preppy drag, executive drag... they even get dressed up in a 'drag' of the sort of streetwear worn by people who, we are told, physically harass them on the regular. They try to perfectly emulate people who exclude or oppress them, and get spangly prizes for doing so. Emulating perfectly is known as 'serving realness', and doing so very perfectly will be said to make the viewer 'gag' with impressedness. And there's something incredible about that to me: that they're claiming something of the world that rejects them; saying 'I can do you better than you' that's sad, gorgeous and fierce.

It says something pretty intense about surface; what's on the surface can unlock worlds and take them away, and that that process can change what's on the inside. Which we obvs knew already, but the way it's messed about with here is so playful and complicated. The aforementioned RuPaul's own mantra "We're all born naked and the rest is drag" goes all-out, that all dress, learnt behaviour and personae we use to engage with the world are inherently absurd and deserve to be played with. Realising this can free you to look behind the Wizard's curtain in Oz, or unplug yourself from the Matrix (she is well into *The Matrix* and *The Wizard of Oz* and talks about them a fair bit, btw. I'm not just intuiting all of this) and then you can be like the people at the end of those films, and fly around in a coat or have teleporting shoes or whatever. And I find that fierce and inspirational. Fiercepirational.

'Fierce', by the way (and I'll stop saying fierce in a minute, promise) is another of the words in the wordage I was talking about. In this context, I think it basically means 'fierce', but fiercer and with topnotes of self-possession...

37 This happened on their honeymoon in Paris, and the window in question was that of *Van Cleef & Arpels*, and he went in and bought everything that could be seen, and then made her wear it to the races. This reduced her to tears, understandably, as doing a Christmas Tree impression under duress is not everybody's cup of tea. It had such an impression on her that in her later years, according to her family, she developed an "obsessive hatred" of jewellery, and only ever wore strings of heavy amber beads. This behaviour, however, was part of an ongoing commitment of Henry's to jewels. He set up a Polish jeweller, Morris Wartski, in a shop in Llandudno and, with his help, began to mainline sparklies with staggering efficiency. It soon became known to the jewellers of Europe that if they acquired a fine specimen, they would always find a buyer in the Marquis of Anglesey. I mean I'd be tempted to be creative with this formula: "Here, Henry, look at this Koh-I-Noor: priceless, one of a kind, comes in a set of two. Hearts of the Ocean! Any bowl £10."

38 Allegedly yes. For example as mentioned in Christopher Sykes, Lilian's grandson's *The Aristocracy – Born to Rule 1875 – 1945*, BBC, 29 Jan 1997. Citation achieved!

39 She did, after being married six weeks, while on their honeymoon. As this is not the last we'll see of Lilian, I'll save the bulk of her *9 to 5*-style 'what she did after' bit for the end. However, we have tweaked the timeline a bit here: as far as I know, she hadn't fallen in love with anyone else at this point, though she would later. In the immediate aftermath of being with Henry, she went very pleasingly off the rails. By the standards of the day, she went off

the rails, off the train, off the gap, off the platform and even off the branch of *Pumpkin* lurking on the station concourse, keenly poised to devastate travellers with a mild-yet-ultimately-quite-draining sense of disappointment with the world. She went full Bohemian, moved into a flat in Ovington Gardens in London where she "dabbled in clever people – actresses, artists and the like" as a friend put it, quoted in Christopher Sykes's *The Visitors' Book*. Sykes continues: "She was soon said to be receiving numerous lovers, sometimes as many as two or three a night", as well as spending a lot of time in Paris, where she would "sip champagne from slippers and dance on tables." You (and I mean this with utmost profundity) go girl.

However, there does seem to have been a bit of a PR gambit done at some point, as *The Des Moines Register* says of her "The countess is a woman of strong religious convictions. Her husband's fondness for the stage and some of the persons on it were repugnant to her. At all events they agreed to a formal separation, the countess going to Paris, where she devoted herself largely to religious work." Despite this, her reputation as a bit of no good never really left her. But more on her later.

40 On the 13th of October, 1898. Ascending to Marquisity of course meant that Henry had access to the motherlode of Paget cash, so he could now go fully bonkers and like build a real Death Star made out of just paté and amethysts. Or stuff like that.

41 He did in fact put on *Henry V*, which I really, really hope was because it was his name and number.

42 It is said that Henry went to London and saw some actors in a show and then offered them double the money they were on to come and be his actors, which is presumably fairly annoying for anyone with tickets for the following night's show who'd already booked their table at Garfunkel's for the pre-theatre special and everything. There were additional benefits for the actors in coming to Plas Newydd, as *The Baltimore Sun* put it: "The professional theatrical people enjoyed themselves hugely in the palace. The change from one-night stands, cheap hotels and the other features of itinerant theatrical life to this abode of luxury, where they had the best of everything to eat and drink and an army of liveried menials to wait on them, was at least as wonderful as any transformation ever produced by Aladdin's magic lamp.

These careless Bohemians supped on champagne, lobsters and Welsh rarebit in the wainscoted hall, where the portraits of a hundred Pagets frowned down upon them. 'Cheer up old boy,' said a merry ballet girl, as she aimed a glass of wine at the head of an Elizabethan gentleman." Which I'm assuming meant like she was cheers-ing the portrait, not flinging booze at it, though who can fully tell. We did experiment with having the Actors played by Keith as hand puppets, or at least by Keith making mouths with his hands. I liked the idea that Keith might get envious of or competitive with his own hands, and want to upstage them. Ultimately though, they didn't really add much, though allowed us to explore the interesting and satirical dramatic conceit that actors can be a bit freeloadery and like a free dinner.

43 He did! The demolition of the old chapel was one of his most cardinal sins in the eyes of the family. The Gaiety Theatre, as twas called, was indeed eggshell blue, and was modeled on Sarah Bernhardt's in Paris (Sarah Bernhardt's as in 'The Divine Sarah', the most famous actress of the 19th Century, as opposed to Sandra Bernhardt, who is different), seating 150 if they all breathed carefully, with a royal box where the organ loft wasn't any more.

44 This is fact. The trail of flaming torches went from the door of the Gaiety to the town square of Llanfairpwllgwyngyllgogerychwyrndrobwllllantysiliogogogoch, the village I mentioned in the Foreword and which I just typed again because I wanted to see if I could type it all in one go without making a mistake. I couldn't.

45 The Gaiety's opening show – the aforementioned 1902 *Aladdin* of tea towel fame – had, to put it mildly, an ample costume budget. Being as Henry didn't really seem to get the concept of 'costume jewellery', and (obvs) everything had to be covered in sparkle, the jewels on one costume alone were worth £3.4M in 2017 (pre Brexit) pounds, and those used in the whole production were worth just shy of £43M. It is an eyewatering amount. Trying to read that figure off the online inflation calculator just literally made my eyes water, though that might also be all this coffee I just had, or a sign that I need some more coffee.

Anyway, Henry, given that his upbringing had given him an understanding of the value of money equivalent to that of a minor deity, took the unutterable expensiveness of it all completely in his stride, and would apparently just leave these costumes in the dressing room unguarded. At one point, Henry's French valet, Julian Gault, stole a bunch of them and made his way for the coast. When he was arrested at Dover, he said that he had been instructed to steal the jewels by a French woman of his acquaintance named Mathilde. Which is a Season Ten sort of storyline if ever I heard one.

Another tale of valety jewel theft, on the other hand, reeks of spinoff potential: "He was staying at a London hotel and one evening while he was out seeing William Gillette play 'Sherlock Holmes', his third valet stole all his jewelry. When the Marquis found out his loss he modeled his actions upon Sherlock Holmes and sent out his friends to track the thief. They caught him and recovered most of the jewels. From the evidence at the trial it appeared that the Marquis wore gold and jeweled bangles around his ankles, diamond belts, diamond stomachers and other ornaments more or less noticeable. All that seemed lacking were earrings and a nosering." (*The Baltimore Sun*, 1902)

But, back to the Gaiety; that same article gives a colourful idea of Henry the entertainer: "Later, the Marquis appeared as a ballet girl, wearing short skirts. He was heavily rouged and he sang a song in a simpering female voice. He has long been known as a very successful female impersonator. He also sang some American coon songs." – the last bit of which doesn't reflect well on anyone concerned.

Meanwhile it continues with a Lilian cameo (surprise!): "As a result of this entertainment the Marquis' beautiful young wife has left him. This is not very surprising, because she left him once before... Two years ago she secured an annulment of the marriage on grounds that were heard in secret. To everybody's astonishment, she applied last year for a rescinding of the annulment, which was granted... She can hardly ask for another annulment."

46 Sadly not factual.

47 This is a reference to the 90s real-time strategy map buildy buildy tanky blowup game *Command & Conquer* where a computer voice goes "construction is complete" when you finish a barracks or whatever. The list of people who enjoy this reference is: me, Matthew (Keith) and Alex (director).

48 This is a gentle stretch of the truth; there are accounts that they were very sparsely attended. There are other accounts that friends came from Liverpool and Manchester to fill it out on occasion.

49 Flyers do definitely always work, and are convivially received by people everywhere, especially during the Edinburgh Fringe. It is known. The one day I semi-successfully flyered during *How to Win*'s run there in 2016, I made eye contact with a lovely-looking family who would definitely love the show, and duly strode towards them, picking my way through quite a lot of picnics on my journey, only for an unseen agent to open a portaloo door nearby as I was just upon them, giving me a heady smack of p-loo whiff directly in my nose and mouth, which made me gag and snarl convulsively. So, from their point of view, some unpleasant git had walked over to them with purpose from quite far away with the sole intention of facially expressing how repulsive he found them. And my face was on the flyer, so the git's identity was totally traceable.

50 There was a section here where Keith rhapsodised about the joys of touring: "Living off nothing but Scotch eggs and applause; staying in grotty digs with an angry landlady called Dotty Griggs and she's got wandering hands and she was in a play once and she'll tell you all about it. Getting up at the crack of dawn with only one clean pair of pants between you and you don't know which one it is."

51 So, IRL the tours sound incredible. The travelling company numbered fifty, including its own orchestra. They had their own painted backdrops, as well as set furniture which were perfect replicas of furniture from Plas Newydd, since Henry would rehearse in his own living room and then only be able to reproduce the performance if surrounded by identical furniture.

The baggage travelled in five trucks, while the personnel travelled in a fleet of cars, all customised to look like the carriages of the Orient Express, featuring carved wood ceilings complete with Rococo cherubs on the inside. To cap it off, the cars, or at least Henry's own, were customised also so that the exhaust fumes were scented with rose petals.

52 The company did indeed present *An Ideal Husband*, in which Henry played Lord Goring. In the words of the actual Alexander Keith: "the part might have been written for him, he went through it so naturally." Others who were not as much in the Marquis's immediate employ, however, for example *The Illustrated Mail* of Bournemouth, felt differently: "The public hardly seemed to take this laudable ambition any more seriously than they did Lord Anglesey's impersonation of Lord Goring, and their reception of the piece was not enthusiastic."

53 The idea of the shows getting gradually more opaque and weird as the tours go on isn't true as such, though he had been performing perplexing work in Berlin prior to this point (of which more later). Also, I don't know that Henry ever played a dog per se, but in Aladdin, "The noble Marquis himself played the role of Pekoe, a sort of monkey with almost human intelligence" (*The Baltimore Sun*). He did, however, have a great number of dogs. Thirty were listed for sale in the auction he had when he ran out of cash. Selected names were: Mora, Queenie, Black Valentine and, curiously, Marquis. One of the dogs is described in the auction's lots list as "fine and upstanding", and another as "not entire".

54 This is a fleeting reference to David Cronenberg's 1986 film *The Fly*, where Jeff Goldblum accidentally fuses himself with a housefly in a teleporter and gradually mutates into a grotesque hybrid. Classic 'Blum. He announces near the end: "I'm an insect who dreamed he was a man and loved it. But now the dream is over and the insect is awake." Which I enjoyed as a way of foreshadowing stuff, what with the butterfly in the next scene, and how Henry sees it as the emergence of something from deep inside him.

55 Aestheticism was an art movement that said that the most important thing was for things to be beautiful; that art had a responsibility to promote beauty rather than morality or politics, and that art, in its artificiality, could be perfect in a way that nature couldn't. They became associated with the quite annoying slogan 'Art for Art's Sake'. Big swingers include Aubrey Beardsley, Oscar Wilde and Dante Gabriel Rossetti. I wouldn't quote me on this, but the whole thing doesn't feel a billion miles away from that tendency in modern art leading up to the work of painters like Rothko and Pollock, where it's supposed to not be about the painting representing anything, but about you, the painting-looker-at, communing with the painting in its special live, in-the-room-with-you paintingyness. With the crucial difference that those kinds of things are all about being butch, gestural, primal, totemic, whereas Aestheticism is about being all gorgeous all the time and there are often peacocks. At least, that's how I recall it from art school lectures, though I have a condition (it's a condition) wherein I fall asleep very easily to the sound of a projector.

56 Lord Berners (aka Gerald Hugh Tyrwhitt-Wilson, 14th Baron Berners) was a contemporary of Henry's (being 1883-1950) and a classical composer, novelist, painter and Lord. He was also exhaustingly wacky. I don't know why, it's total prejudice I guess, but I find his eccentricities deeply tiresome while I don't Henry's. For some reason I just don't buy them. Like, listen: his garden had paper flowers in it; he once had Penelope Betjeman's horse round for tea; he built a tower then put a sign on it saying "Members of the public committing suicide from this tower do so at their own risk"; he responded to being told that you could teach a dog to swim if you throw it in water by throwing a dog out the window to see if it would learn to fly; he drove around his estate in a pig's head mask to frighten the locals... and so on and so on.

While staying as open as possible to the idea that everyone is special and deserves to express their needs and feelings in whatever way seems best to them and all that, I do feel like there's a difference between being a true eccentric and just being a knob. He may well not have been a knob, and anyway, who am I to cast the first knob? But I find it interesting to note the similarities between Berners and Henry: both considered eccentrics, both involved in the arts, both Lords, both had modified wackymobiles i.e. Berners had a car with a built-in clavichord in it. But also the differences: Berners was respected, a polymath, had Salvador Dalí, H.G. Wells and Igor Stravinsky round his house; he had an acknowledged sexuality and romantic identity, having explored his gayness at Eton, where he developed a relationship with an older boy that only ended when Berners puked on him for some reason, and in later life had a companion, Robert ('Mad Boy') Heber Percy, to whom he bequeathed his estate.

Of course, Henry might have been comfortable with all manner of aspects of himself that we don't know about, because his internal life got burnt and all that, and he might have actually been very fulfilled and that whole "pathetically alone" comment mentioned in Footnote 10 could have just been the product of homophobic minds failing to comprehend relationships different to their own. We'll never really know, I guess, and the story I've chosen to tell here is just one possibility.

But to wrestle this back to the point: Lord Berners saw Henry perform IRL, and he was very dismissive about it (see Footnote 62). Even worse than when Lulu – name drop, clang, sorry – saw us do a couple of songs from this show at a party and then she and I had an awkward pas de deux in the corridor by the toilet, and she politely said well done and she thought we must have "worked very hard on it". And I think that's a bit sad (not the Lulu thing; I'm over it – I was never that into *The Man with the Golden Gun* anyway) because in my insipid mind I think Henry and Berners could have been kindred squirrelfriends, and they weren't. But maybe if I had actually seen Henry perform I'd have thought he was a knob too. Maybe we're all knobs.

57   Roland the apricot is made up as far as I know, though Berners did used to feed people peaches, and when people said they were nice, he'd say "Yes, they are ham-fed."... I mean isn't he *exhausting??*

58   The specific kind of avant garde music this is a reference to is the 2nd Viennese School whose big guns included Arnold Schoenberg who I had to study at school, and whose work does involve quite a lot of energetic key-whackage and strangly noises.

59   Now, blatantly we got this German phrase through Google Translate, but we checked it with several actual Germanfolk, and they thumbsed it up. A few people have said that we pronounce it wrong, and the truth is by this point I'd written the song and needed it to rhyme with "hurt", "dessert" and "Kurt", so I was motivated to have it be pronounced that way. However, I'm not mercenary enough a narcissist to demand the alteration of an entire language just to save me having to rewrite three lines, so I was delighted to speak to an East German specifically, who said that in the East German accent (and crucially Dresden is *in* East Germany), it is pronounced thus. A lucky break for me, and a lucky escape too for German speakers everywhere, who can continue to speak their language as they always have, without knowing how close they came.

60 The *Butterfly Dance*, sometimes the *Electric Butterfly Dance* and on special occasions *The Famous Electric Butterfly Dance* was Henry's calling card, performed under the pseudonym Sun Toi, which was a character in a contemporary musical comedy. He'd do it as a standalone in music halls, or work it into other shows as an interlude on a pretty ad hoc scattergun basis, regardless of context. He did it in Act 5 of The Gaiety's *Aladdin*, for example, which I suppose makes as much sense as the pantomime *Aladdin* being traditionally set in China (why is that anyway?). Good old *Baltimore Sun* again: "He introduced a butterfly dance in a gorgeous costume, covered with £250,000 worth of the historical Anglesey jewels. He wore enormous butterfly wings, with antennae on his head, and all the other features of this graceful insect," while a Berlin paper (which I can't find the name of) said of his show performed there "In a dark house on a dark stage he produces kaleidoscopic pictures in lifesize... The splendour and brightness of the colours, the tasteful combination, and the constant change of the beautiful electric light on the slender form of the artist, clothed in white, gladdened the eyes."

It's possible that it was inspired by the work of Loie Fuller, an American dancer and theatrical lighting pioneer, who had recently made famous *The Serpentine Dance*, in which she makes ingenious use of floaty fabric, some sticks and the concept of waving things around to create lovely shapes as a sort of platonic ideal version of Kate Bush, or like Tim Curry's Grand Wizard Halloween dance in the amazing *The Worst Witch* with Diana Rigg and Fairuza Balk and Tim Curry, which if you look at it has *got* to be a direct homage. Fuller was filmed doing it by them early cinematographers the Lumière Brothers, which you can see on Youtube. Or, like, if you have a magic lantern or a zoetrope or whatever you'd watch 1900s movies on.

61 This whole section is a conscious coupling of a couple of different events, drawn together, and moulded into the story that we wanted to tell. The first element is the *Butterfly Dance* itself, as described above in Footnote 60. The second is rather odder, and is described in Footnote 62.

62 What he actually said, in his memoir, entitled *Dresden*, was: "I had heard that Lord Anglesey had previously appeared in other Continental music halls, and that all he did was to show himself in the family jewels. It didn't sound to me a very exciting performance; however, in spite of Mrs Mansfield's injunction, I was determined to go and see it.

If not exactly exciting it was decidedly a strange "turn". It came between that of a lady with performing pigeons and a company of acrobats. The theatre was darkened. There was a roll on the drums and the curtain went up on Lord Anglesey clad in a white silk tunic, a huge diamond tiara on his head, glittering with necklaces, brooches, bracelets and rings. He stood there for a few moments motionless, without any mannequin gestures of display.

Then the curtain went down again period. No applause followed, only an animated buzz of conversation. The German audience seemed a little disconcerted by the manifestation of British eccentricity, I may say that German audiences even in the music halls were extremely disciplined and well-behaved. Once at the Dresden opera a new tenor, appearing for the first time in the role of Lohengrin, missed his footing on stepping out of the swan-boat and fell headlong on the stage. His shield and helmet were restored to him by members of the chorus, and the performance was resumed in perfect silence. There was not a sound of the faintest chuckle. Lord Anglesey, I thought, had got off lightly.

Imagine the reception of such a display by an English music hall audience. The press treated the matter with similar restraint. The critics merely commented on the magnificence of the jewels."

... which I reckon pretty much amounts to the same.

63 Henry was declared bankrupt on the 11th June 1904 and all of his stuff – cars, dogs, the lot – got flogged in the 'Anglesey Sales', a vast season of auctions which drew crowds over the more than 40 days that it took to cash-in-the-attic the 17,000 lots. The three days it took to sell his clothes were the most popular, and developed a carnival atmosphere, as reported in the *Evening Post*, 5th Nov 1904:

"The sale opened with a somewhat sensational duel between the London 'ring' (of dealers) and a Bangor broker for the possession of a sky-blue silk bath-gown. Ladies murmured that it was very pretty and thought they would go up to a guinea for it, but in a sharp volley of ten-shilling bids the price rose to £8 10s, at which the Bangor man was content to stop. "Upon my word and honour," said Mr Drew, the auctioneer, in good spirits at such a start, "you must want a bath very much." Mr Drew there, potentially confusing 'a bathrobe' and 'a bath'.

The *Chicago Tribune* was pretty scathing about the whole thing: "Anglesey Sales Huge Joke" it announced; "The sale of the marquis of Anglesey's collection of treasures at Anglesey castle has been creating more amusement than excitement, and lots have been going simply dirt cheap. The marquis's reputation for eccentricity did not lose by yesterday's revelations. There was no need for the auctioneer's witticisms. The grotesque waistcoats and suits provoked laughter in themselves... Some of the smoking jackets would have shamed Joseph's famous garment." Nice musical theatre reference, *CT*.

That article then goes on to gush about canes with the enthusiasm of Violet Berlin presenting *Bad Influence*, but about cane tech instead of 90s Virtual Reality or cheats for *Cosmic Spacehead* or whatever: "One beautifully chased knob exhibits in the crown a watch of the best Parisian make. Though no larger than a farthing, it is sown with jewels. Touch a spring and the watch revolves to disclose an exquisite miniature portrait of a lady. Of the eccentric and bizarre there is much. A beautifully modeled cockatoo's head becomes lifelike at the touch of a spring. One silver head of Malacca contains a perfect little snapshot camera, and another conceals a battery which at a touch sets tiny bulbs aglow with electric light." I'm really not sure how to picture a cockatoo that "becomes lifelike at the touch of a spring" – it's conceivable the author just prodded an actual cockatoo that was sitting on a cane.

In any case, the whole dog and pony show (there were probably ponies, let's face it) didn't really raise as much money as Henry's creditors would have hoped for; the *Tribune* later reported that they "received 1.5 cents on the dollar".

This whole section, tragically, is a fantasy. We wanted a satisfying end to Keith's story, and needed to up the stakes for Henry's 'darkest hour' turnaround in Monte Carlo. I mean I say that, but mainly what we needed was that bit in the musical where everything is weaving together and people are urgently shouting bits of previous songs over each other, like 'One Day More' from *Les Mis* or the far more successful pisstake of it in *South Park: Bigger, Longer and Uncut*, 'La Resistance'. In the end, this song doesn't do that as much as I'd intended, in fact one of the main songs it references ("How to Be in Control", which is printed elsewherem in this book) has been cut anyway. Oh well, ho hum and so on.

64 This is a reference to *Smash*, which is the most important piece of television created in the last ten years. It's about a the all-singing, all-hoofing, all-making-no-sense misadventures of a ragtag band of established theatre professionals putting on a Broadway show about Marilyn Monroe. Anyway, there's way too much to say about it, but Matthew (Mr Keith) and I were obsessed with it.

As was the producer, Áine. Her career template is Anjelica Huston's character in it, who is a brassy, no-nonsense Broadway producer with helmet hair, shoulderpads and an immovable face, who spends most of her screen time contriving to throw martinis in her evil ex-husband's face, in a variety of ways which range from the comical to the poignant.

So Áine would often be found during rehearsals reclining along the back row, with a stopwatch and a clipboard, piping up occasionally with "Yous guys know you've gone seven minutes there without a song, and people like songs, and momma loves ticket money and I've got forty pink flamingoes on pre-order for the Broadway run and the deposit's non-refundable so."

Actually, Áine and I knew we were going to get on when we first met to discuss working together, spent about ten minutes talking about this show, and then about an hour talking about *Smash*. That and the fact that she once infiltrated the dressing room of the pivotal girl group *Cleopatra* under the pretence of being the photographer for a fictitious Irish gay magazine, and thus has in her possession a memory card full of completely unique shots of them. In fact, come to think of it, I believe part of the deal of this whole thing was that I'd get to see them. Excuse me while I make a mental note to immediately attend to that.

65 For non Welshophones, here is a translation:
Herd, come, attend, o knot of Welshfolk,
I appear among you like a spectre.
I am now going to say the word "astronaut" for no reason.
Do not prattle; shushy. For I...
... am Keith

66 This is a near-quote from the last episode of *Buffy the Vampire Slayer*, which is my favourite thing, and I consider it a sign of my personal growth that I've only put in one explicit *Buffy* reference in here. Anyway, she says it when she realises that (spoiler-free version) in order to win the final battle, she's going to have to turn the whole concept of her world on its head. Which is sort of what Henry does here. Without an oddly chrome axe and Alyson Hannigan.

67 Cerdd Dant is a discipline which exists solely in Wales. Basically, you've got your harp, you've got a folk tune and you've got a poem. The harp plays the same short-to-medium lengthed tune over and over again, and you have to sing the poem over the top of it in a countermelody, while not singing the same melody twice. And then once you find that easy, you do it in four-part harmony. I mean for that you do get to have other people to help you, unless you have multiple voice-pipes like the Diva from *The Fifth Element*. But anyway, so me doing a sort of cod version of it for a handful of lines is a piece of cheesecake in comparison.

But the real thing, when it works, sounds woven and gorgeous and innately pleasing like a love spoon or the cross section of a Viennetta. When it doesn't, it sounds like two people booked the same room to rehearse in at the same time and neither of them will back down.

While we're on the subject of Welsh culture, according to the Welsh-language paper *Y Cymro (The Welshman)* of the 16th March 1905, Henry had been part of the Gorsedd, or Throne of Bards, which is a sort of a Welsh Language Culture Honours System where you have different ranks of bards in druidic robes rising in status from green through blue to white. Reports from the Anglesey Sales say that two special silk bardic cloaks from Henry's induction into the Gorsedd, in crimson and green silk, were among the cheapest things sold.

When you're inducted, you pick yourself a bardic name. Henry chose the name "Cadrawd Hardd". Cadrawd is the name of a 6th century King of Calchfynydd – I guess 'Chalk Mountain' – an obscure ancient British kingdom mentioned in the medieval Book of Taliesin. Cadrawd is referred to as one of the "men of the north", which is literally v *Game of Thrones*. And 'hardd' is an adjective; there's no prizes for guessing which one if you remember the whole aesthete thing, but it rhymes with 'fluteyful' and it's not 'dutiful'.

68 The melody in the first line of this stanza is a brief reference to *Nessun Dorma* from the Puccini opera *Turandot*, which I put in cos:

(a) I think it's pretty

(b) In the opera, the character singing it is looking out at night over a kingdom that's in chaos, because he's made a bet with its princess that she can't guess his name before the break of day and she's furiously sent all her subjects out to search for the answer. He climaxes (the song) by yelling "At dawn, I will win!"; so something about being really pleased with yourself while not sleeping – as well as something about people knowing or not knowing your name – seemed appropriate

(c) Pointlessly convoluted easter eggs are pleasing to me.

69   This quote, from "I must…" to "…Scotch Tweed." is verbatim, and it is from
      a genuine *Daily Mail* interview. It's one bit of solid Henry that exists and, for
      me, this quote is what made me want to tell this story. I mean obviously I'd
      have a lovely time poncing about in sparkles pretending to be any number
      of historical characters / women with the surname Zbornak, but this quote
      is what made Henry's story richer than that.

      The reply of the journalist character (who probably wasn't really called Quentin:
      Quentin is just a name we generated randomly for the character, because we
      didn't want to take the opportunity to take a cheap shot at any particular real
      life *Daily Mail* journalists, whose commitment to their work is ceaseless and
      unremitting, like ants, or Polonium-210) is also practically verbatim from "I am
      astonished…" to "… exaggerated." except for one slight edit for clarity.

      The *Mail* believes what Henry says. Although it's *definitely* a lie. I mean he
      definitely, defiantly did like wearing dresses; I mean it's mathematically
      impossible that anyone could accidentally trip and fall into that many
      fabulous frocks. The thing about it is that it shows a sharp awareness:
      Henry's aware that the journalist – and the world he represents – expects
      something of him, so he plays the part. For one blazing moment, he passes
      as respectable; he serves acceptable ruling class realness, and he makes the
      Daily Mail gag on it. And whether that act of 'passing' is the ultimate victory
      or the ultimate defeat is really up for grabs. But either way, it felt pricklily
      political, sexy, subversive and totally queer.

      It made me want to make this story about pretending, realness, camp and
      the complex, unfathomable challenge of "being yourself".

70   Lilian – despite having left Henry, then returned to him briefly, and then
      left again – returned to him for the end. From the *Weekly News*, March 17th
      1905: "According to a Monte Carlo correspondent, a reconciliation between
      the Marquis and the Marchioness took place on Monday, and Lady Anglesey
      was with his Lordship to the last… Besides the Marchioness, his Lordship's
      aunt was also with him before death supervened."

71   Lilian, following her days in Paris and Bloomsbury living the religious life,
      with many actors a night, sipping champagne from plimsolls – or whichever
      combination of those facts you care to believe – and despite returning to
      Henry for the end, would never speak of her time with him again. In fact,
      according to her grandson, Christopher Sykes, in his *The Visitors' Book*
      (which is where much of this bit comes from), the closest she came was
      when her friend Jo Churston brought it up in later, happier years, and Lilian
      replied, "Once you've sailed your boat into the harbour, Jo, you don't take it
      out again."

      I mean, little as I know about shipping, I'm fairly sure that's not true. If it
      were, all harbours would just be full of boats that have done one trip then
      retired, which scarcely seems very efficient. But the sentiment is pretty
      poignant. She renounced all the jewels he'd given her, but she did keep a set
      of hairbrushes and hand mirrors with huge Anglesey coronets on them.

Her reputation was mud at this point, though presumably fairly sparkly mud: I imagine being with Henry is a bit like opening a Christmas card with glitter in it, and then you have glitter somewhere on you always for life. In fact, Lady Morrison-Bell was told by someone who found out she and Lilian were becoming friends: "You shouldn't go near that woman; you can't touch pitch without catching some smear." Which is basically the same analogy.

In 1909 she became engaged with John Gilliatt, a dishy, sporty, charming, musiciany banker seven years her junior, and with whom she was in love reciprocatedly, but this didn't help with the whole rep thing. As husband and wife, they went once to a party at which also was King George V and Queen Mary. Following the party, Queen Mary wrote to the hostess to thank her profusely, but finished by asserting "we did not enjoy meeting Mrs Gilliatt." I mean, a monarchial bitch-slap like that is what *Downton Abbey* season finales are made of.

Lilian decided to stop caring. With Jack (Jack is the same person as John), she built a new life, still among theatricals. They became known for the help they would give to up-and-coming musicians and entertainers, through showcase parties. One of the struggling young things they gave a leg up to turned out to be Noël Coward. I mean presumably he already was Noël Coward, but you know what I mean.

They had three children: John, Simon and Virginia. Simon, an RAF pilot, was killed when his plane crashed on take off in 1936. His brother, who was also in the plane, attempted to save him. John himself died eight years later when a chapel service he was in was bombed. When Lilian heard the news, her friend Denise Ebury said "she let out a long, drawn-out groan of despair that I shall never forget." Jack then died four years later, on a golf course, sources say he'd just played his best stroke ever.

But Virginia survived, and begat Christopher, who was such a help when I was writing this show, as was his daughter, my friend Lily. And it wasn't until embarrassingly late on that I realised who she's named after.

72 Henry died on the 14th of March 1905, He was then brought back home to Anglesey to be buried. "The coffin, enclosed in a packing-case, was brought from Paris through the night, unaccompanied by any relatives or friends, nor was there anyone at the Victoria Station of the London, Brighton and South Coast line to receive the remains except the railway officials and undertaker's staff," said the *Evening Express*, March 23rd. It then goes on to describe in peculiar amounts of detail the ceremony whereby the insurance company opened the coffin to check it was him, given the value of the policy on his life. Then "It was understood that the coffin would be taken to Llanfair PG, and thence to the chapel at Plas Newydd, to remain there until the hour of the burial."

Now, of course, at this point there was no chapel at Plas Newydd. It may just be the paper's mistake, but I like the idea that he spent his last hours above ground lying in the Gaiety Theatre.

And quite a lot of ink would be spilled over that little body. Most of it, as we've been over, not great: two-star reviews at best. "Pathetic close to a 'Butterfly Career'" said *The Cambrian*, "A Wasted Life" said the *Evening Express*. But there are some other intriguing accounts. Like this one from *The Welsh Coast Pioneer*:

" 'I saw him,' writes one who has followed his career with some amount of attention, "two or three years ago in London. Of all the extraordinary dandies which the pictures of a century ago has left on record, none eclipsed the young Marquis of Anglesey. His whole appearance was unusual and bizarre. He wore a mixture of colours, which attracted attention at once, and then the blaze of diamonds kept the eye captive. But his face was vacuous and pale, and his attitude was of an 'old young man' bored with existence." In appearance the marquis had a decidedly foreign look, and his taste in some matters were finely critical. There was, however, an almost total absence of the masculine quality in his character, and he went with easy facility from one extravagance to others greater still."

However, the article then continues; "Obscured as it was by many foibles and vulgarities, there was a trait in the Marquis of Anglesey's character which merited more recognition than it obtained, and that was his charity. Whenever a needy case was mentioned to him he immediately proffered assistance. The only condition he imposed was that his gifts should be kept a profound secret."

Backed up by this from the *Evening Express* (the "wasted life" one): "The news of the death of the marquess caused much regret at Bangor, as the marquess, despite his peculiarities, was much liked. The principal shops of Bangor have drawn their blinds." and this, from *The Weekly News*: "Despite his weaknesses, Lord Anglesey holds a warm place in the memories of at least his Welsh tenants, for he was a kindly hearted man and a model landlord."

I'd like to quote a bit more of that article, actually, as it gives good recap, but with a hefty dose of 1900s pomp: "And so has death removed one of the most romantic and interesting figures of our time – a man who gratified every fancy in the most extravagant manner, who bought diamonds as an ordinary man buys cigarettes, who filled every corner of his rooms with exquisite souvenirs and jewelled bijouterie, who wedded a young and beautiful woman and separated from her when their married life had hardly begun, who hired a comic opera troupe to live at Anglesey Castle at double salaries, who became bankrupt on an income of £100,000 a year; and with it all was half a philosopher. But death has intervened. Destiny has not allowed the Marquis's plans for a newer – and may be for a more useful – life to materialise."

The funeral was apparently quite a simple affair, a handful of people at Llanedwen Church, where Anglesey Marquisi tend to be buried. The *Evening Express* again: "On the coffin were placed two beautiful wreaths and a cross, whilst a lady attired in deep mourning also deposited a bunch of white flowers."

A final mini cameo for Lilian? I can only speculate, but I can totally picture the scene with her in it, and behind her, shimmering, the two ghosts from Eton, like Yoda and Obi Wan in *Return of the Jedi*.

73 So, there we are. As I said, there is a bunch more about Henry than what made it into the show. Some of it might go back in if we decide to Peter Jackson the whole thing into an extended edition. But, as is the way of things, a lot of it is contradictory, a lot of it belongs in a different telling of his story, a lot of it is speculation and a lot of it is, as far as I can tell, empirically just not true and may be a typo. Like, I found one newspaper that said that Henry Cyril Paget, 5th Marquis of Anglesey was the son of Henry Cyril Paget, 5th Marquis of Anglesey. Which, unless we conclude that this universe is being written by Steven Moffat, probably isn't canon.

The beauty of his story is, for me, that it's hollow. I don't mean hollow like "oh my god modern life is so phoney, why do we even bother to read books and have kids and brush our teeth anyway, everything's so fake, emo emo emo", but hollow like you can pour yourself into it, or try it on, like (oh my god, I just gave myself ten points) a *dress*.

We have so few of his actual words, his internal voice; all we have is a series of amazing things that he did, and we don't really know what he was thinking at any point while he was doing them. Maybe if we did, he wouldn't be so fascinating. Maybe if we did, we wouldn't like him at all. So, thanks fire. Thanks, patriarchy. You've turned him into a legend.

But we do have fragments of his words, and whenever I read them I read into them the glassy, friendly optimism, with something flickering inside, that I've tried to build this show around. To finish, here's a quote I hadn't read until quite recently, but which encompasses quite a lot of those characteristics I find so appealing. It's from just before he went to Monte Carlo:

"Interviewed on his departure he smiled a little bitterly, and while admitting that 'luckily it isn't given everyone to be blessed with such an entourage and such friends as I have enjoyed; however, I've learnt my lesson. My misfortunes are only temporary,' he added cheerfully, 'and can soon be repaired. The sales seem to have gone well, and the removal of some of the furniture is half a blessing in disguise. A good deal of it required replacing.' "
– *The Weekly News*, March 17th, 1905

WING COLLAR
LOOSE TIE

BROOCH ON
LAPEL

NON WOOL
WAISTCOAT

WATCH LINK
CHAIN

HIGH WAISTED
TROUSERS

BROGUES

MR. KEITH

MAN AGAINST HISTORY

THEATRE
VERITY QUINN
DESIGNER

WING COLLAR
& BOSS BOWTIE OR
LOOSE CRAVAT

POCKET SQUARE

BLACK TAILS
& WAISTCOAT

CUMMABAND

FRILLY CUFFS

TASSLES AT
HEM

BREECHS &
WHITE TIGHTS

WINKLEPICKERS

HOW TO BUILK AGAINST HISTORY

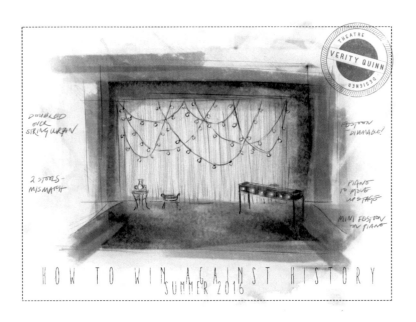

THEATRE
VERITY QUINN
DESIGNER

DOUBLED OVER STRING URBAN

2 STOOLS - MISMATCH

FESTOON DIMMABLE!

PIANO TO MOVE UPSTAGE

MINI FESTOON ON PIANO

HOW TO WIN AGAINST HISTORY
SUMMER 2016

CUT SONG 1
'NOBODY REALLY KNOWS'

About it:

This was a song originally done by the ghosts after 'The Prophecy' when asked to be a bit more specific. The idea was that they were both actually quite new to prophetic ghosting as a job, and were just sort of styling it out.

This let us play with that thing that when you're young, you think the world is all this sorted out place full of people who know what they're doing and you're just really mixed up, but then as you get older you realise that everyone's normally in the same state of chaotic paddling to try and keep up this veneer of competence; which is simultaneously reassuring and pretty terrifying.

In the end, it was cut for length and because at the time we couldn't make it work without slowing things down when you need them to whoosh forward. Which is a shame because it was a real breakout bit for Band, which Tom (Penn, who played Band at the time) did just stunningly; and the "Everybody lives, everybody dies" bit was one of my favourites.

H: So, did you have some, like, actual advice?

K: Oh...

B: Don't worry, I've got this.

Gospel Pop.

Free and sparkling to begin with, HENRY and KEITH doing oohs like in 'Like a Prayer'. A spotlight on BAND.

B: [*muchos vocal gymnastics*]
           Look at us a chattering o-on
           A giving you advice
           What do we know-ooh?
           We were only trying to be nice
           Just making random noises – *boop boop scattety boop!*
           Like some mice playin' di-i-ice
           And now we've probs gone and
           Psychologically scarred you for life
KB: Our bad.
K: The thing is

Bouncy pulse, building with their refrain.

KB: We don't really know what we're doing
We don't really know what we're doing
We don't really know what we're doing
We! Don't! Know what we're doing!

B: So here's the thing!

Slightly latin, like the aforementioned 'Like a Prayer' or to an extent '(I've Had) The Time of My Life' from that film about a watermelon.

B: It is easy in this world
To develop the hypothesis
That everybody else you see around you
Is totally on top of it all
And you start to get to thinking
In your pocket of existence
You must have had a cystic infection
Or something
The day everybody else was handed out instructions

KB: On life

KB: It isn't so, isn't so
No!

HKB: Dah-da-da-duh-dah-da

HENRY is finding himself joining in. It's like the infectious rhythm is seducing him! (if that doesn't sound creepy it being about a young boy and all).

B: There's really only so much
You can get from education

K: *Booky booky spooky spooky ooh*

B: For the real stuff everyone just sort of copies
The previous generation

K: *Of people doing stuff!*

B: It's how a doctor really learns how to doct
And it's how a geisha learns how to geishen
It's how a wigmaker learns to deal with real bad wig situation
And how a taxi driver learns to not like immigration

KB: Copying, copying
Ha!

HKB: Dah-da-da-duh-dah-da

K: It's like you go one day

'Today I wish to bake'
But you've got no written recipe
With which a cake to make
KB: But all you've got is a
Million pictures of cakes
K: It's a bit like that.
B: Or look at your teachers
Here at E-ton
When they were little boys
They were be-aten
So their brain's like 'Hey, I need to turn that boy chartreuse'

B: And in the biz we call that
The cycle of abuse!
HKB: Dah-da-da-duh-dah-da

B: No-body really knows what they're doing
They just hope that you can't tell
KB: And when things are going well
They tryin' not to dwell
On all the lives they're screwing
HKB: Dah-da-da-du-du-duh

B: I can't really play the piano.
[*BAND plays the piano badly*] I mean not really, I get by
K: I didn't know how to be a ghost
Until I took a bunch of drugs and died
And I still don't – that's okay!
And we might never won't
KB: But we'll be damned if we'll let on, just
Imp-ro-vise, imp-ro-vise
Ha!
HKB: Dah-dah-dah-duh
KB: Wooooooooooooooah…

It all gets very clappy and inspirational like Sister Act 2: Back in the Habit, or its prequel, Sister Act.

KB: Everybody lives, everybody dies!
And in the middle you improvise
HKB: Everybody lives, everybody dies!
And in the middle you improvise
Everybody lives, everybody dies, u-huh!

> And in the middle you improvise
> Everybody lives, everybody dies!
> And in the middle you improvise

A capella, with the audience gleefully joining in. BAND leaps out into the middle of the floor and takes it to church. The song, I mean, not the floor.

HKB: Everybody lives, everybody dies!
And in the middle you improvise
Everybody lives, everybody dies!
And in the middle you improvise
Everybody lives, everybody dies, u-huh!
And in the middle you improvise
Everybody lives, everybody dies!
And in the middle you...

The ghosts point to HENRY. He is being given 'the hot hand', and must think fast. He does.

H: [*imporivising*] Profiteroles! Cracqueembouche!
Chocolate cake! ... Non-chocolate cake.
... yoghurt.

He peters out as veryone is looking at him say Bake Off things.

B: ... what are you doing?
H: I'm... improvising...
B: OH!
Check you out you had a go
KB: Just spit it out like a mouth volcano – ha!
HKB: Dah-da-da-du-du-duh

Suddenly small and pretty.

B: No-body really knows what they're saying
They just
KB: [*very clearly carefully planned*] ... improvise!
K: They flap their jaws and eyes
B: And roughly half is lies
KB: And ten percent's just neighing
Ney-neyney-neh-neying

Up tempo again. HENRY is really getting it!

K:	So in order to be you
H:	Just pretend "you" don't exist
K:	Just go out shopping with a "you" shopping list
H:	Look at the row of "you" hats on the "you" promotional shelf
H**K:**	Just pick one out and try it on and woah!
	You're "being yourself"!
HKB:	Dah-da-da-du-du-duh

B:	No-body really knows what they're being
HKB:	That's how we run the biz, so
B:	Blow yourself a kiss
K:	And do try not to miss
HKB:	'Cos this is how the world
	This pretty pretty world
	Remains the way
	It very bloody is!
HB:	Dah-da-da-du-du-duh
	Dah-da-da-du-du-duh
B:	That whole thing was completely off the cuff
K:	Well done

CUT SONG 2
'HOW TO BE IN CONTROL'

About it:
This one's a bit of an epic, a whirling tour through the ancient history of Anglesey and the various ways in which people try to influence the world around them using just belief and pure gumption. The story about the wardancers is actual history btw, the Roman historian Tacitus wrote about it. #research

The song used to be at the point where nobody turns up to the first production at Henry's theatre, and comprised the pep-talk slash acting masterclass Keith gives him in order to convince him to believe in himself and try again, which then led into them taking the show on tour.

It was cut primarily for length, but also because I don't feel we *quite* nailed the way it fit into the story dramatuuuurgically. I want to try and put it back in at some point though, if only because it has an actual dance fight in it, and I mean I mean though. Anyway...

K: Let's see what you've got. Take to the boards forthwith; show me your Henry the Fifth.

HENRY takes up a heroic position with a sword upheld, KEITH takes up a directorly position, i.e. he straddles a chair backwards like a horse or Christine Keeler.

Twinkling, like a meek Noël Coward.

H: Once more unto the breach dear friends
         Once more
K: [*spoken*] Very good...
H: Cry havoc and unleash your little dogs
         Of war
K: [*spoken*] And pause!
         [*sings*] But when you're out there facing all those
         Francophile, Francophone French
         And you flench
H: You may blench
K: Your buttocks clench
H: And you're about to drench your stench
K: Remember these encouraging words I ment-ion:
         "*Many just like you have gone before you,*
         On this very soil; this very island; this other 'other Eden';
         this Anglesey,
         And been perfectly adequate."

A tempo. Soulful pop, a la 'Jesus was a Cross Maker' by Judee Sill.

K: Let me take you back to historical times

H: When rocks were really rocks and drinking water pure

K: There were druids roaming round on Anglesey

H: Doing New Age stuff when that was even newer

They pick out various audience members and indicate that they are the druids.

K: They wore white white robes and they had white white beards

H: Unless their natural shade was blond or brown or ginger or... other

K: And they liked natural things like fish and trees and things

H: And they thought hills were the boobs of the universal earth mother

HK: It was their job to make the sun shine on Wales
Which was tricky
For obvious reasons!

K: So they did what little they could
Sacrificed some virgins

HENRY places a mime virgin on an audience member's lap.

H: [*very, very gently in both sing and stab*] They went stab stab stab stab stab stab

He realises that the sacrifice is un-gagged, and puts his hand on their mouth. Then happily proceeds.

H: ... stab stab stab stab stab stab stab stab

He asks if the audience member can hold the (mime) knife, places his hands in the chest cavity of the mime virgin.

HK: Hold your bloody hands in the air and sing
'Come on, sunshine!'

It is the chorus, and they do a skillful thing where they revolve while doing druidy arm-waving, and the lights make it look like the sun is rising and falling around them.

HK: Look at all the beardy men
Who made it their mission in living
To cause the sun to teleport
Into the correct position, singing
'Dawn, please go on and on
Dawning, please go on
Holy fireball we need your he-eat
But we just
Wanna know
How to be in control!'

K: You see Henry, even here, on this Anglesey – which you do Marquisise – there are countless local historical examples of people who were just like you.

H: What do you mean 'like me'?

K: You know... [*gestures: 'sparkly'*]

H: [*Prickles slightly*] Oh. So, what's another one?

Pause.

An uptick in beat, an edge of disco coming in.

HK: So later on the Celts were fighting
To slow the Roman army's advance
And the secret weapon hidden in the ranks of the Celtic army
Was wild women trained in expressive movement
And dance! Boom!

They strike a variety of excellent Voguey poses.

HKB: Wild women trained in expressive movement
And dance! Boom!
And dance! Boom!
And dance and dance and dance and dance and
HK: And the war-dancing women lined up on the southern shore of the island
And awaited the greatest dance of their lives!

Pause. Tension.

K: And they stood
HKB: There!

H: With woad all over
              Yeah!

K: And urine in their
              Hair!

H: And they looked...
              Mmmhmm.

Music turbulent and Benjamin Britten-y. Or, like, Benjamin Britney.

KEITH becomes the Roman Empire, ideally climbing up into the audience rake.

K: And the Romans arrived on the opposing bank
              And looked over at the frankly insane choreography of their opponents
              Throwing incredible shapes, gleaming in the period Welsh evening sun
              And they danced and they danced and they danced

HENRY is possessed by the very lord of the dance itself, i.e. becomes a mental ball of dances: Charleston, Riverdance, Pina Bausch, Single Ladies...

KEITH fights against it to no avail; an irresistible force meets an immovable fiercedom machine. It is like Professor X versus Magneto, except a bit camp.

H: And the Romans thought that there was

HK: A force field
              Preventing them from getting
              Over the water to slaughter druids

H: And they were having all the worst feels
              And they were like

K: [*a perfect Italian accent*] "Ey who is-a do this? What is-a this-a thing
              [*totally English again*] Called 'sass'?"

They are both Wardancers again, Charlie's Angelsing slash Destiny's Childsing in silhouette.

HKB: Look at all the painted ladies
              Off their faces on delicious visions
              Using dance to halt the advance
              Of the whole damn Roman legion

HK: Singing 'We ladies deride
The way you seem to like to do genocide
We are clearly fiercer than tho-ou
Take a look at our high leg kicks and we will let you know
How to be in control'

Uptick again in energy, it's tipping into Bonnie Tyler territory.

H: So, they were all slaughtered?
K: But what can we learn from savages like that?
H: *Savages like tha-a-at?*
K: Even through the bloodshed they gave it all
HKB: The show went on!
HK: Even centuries later
In this very room we're in
K: Men used ritual
H: Passion
HK: Sparkle,
To lean upon the greatest hand they had
To lean upon...

Suddenly spare, churchy and a bit beautiful.

HKB: Look at all the pious men
Who prayed inside this very chapel
Saying sorry for this one time
This one filly ate an apple, singing
'Father and son, go on and on
Loving, please go on
PS we've got this Empire to run

Badass again: swirling actions, lights, sun rising bright over a sea of Union Flags etc.

HKB: So we juuust wanna knooow
Yeah we juuust wanna knooow
And we run the world so we need to know!
How to be in cont –
How to move the sun!
How to be in control!
Amen!'